LINES OF LIFE RUN THROUGH THE MOUNTAINS

A Message of Hope

Thelma J Flynn

Thelma J. Flynn

ISBN 979-8-89243-674-8 (paperback)
ISBN 979-8-89243-675-5 (digital)

Copyright © 2024 by Thelma J. Flynn

All rights reserved. No part of this publication may be reproduced, distributed, or transmitted in any form or by any means, including photocopying, recording, or other electronic or mechanical methods without the prior written permission of the publisher. For permission requests, solicit the publisher via the address below.

Christian Faith Publishing
832 Park Avenue
Meadville, PA 16335
www.christianfaithpublishing.com

Library of Congress Control Number: 1-13127648841

Printed in the United States of America

Life has a plan for you and me. Will we have the wisdom to implement it?

As we age, we gain experiences, knowledge, and wisdom—knowledge about a topic and the wisdom of when and how to use it.

> For I know the thoughts that I think toward you, saith the Lord, thoughts of peace, and not of evil, to give you an expected end. (Jeremiah 29:11 KJV)

> Now the God of Hope fill you with all joy and peace in believing, that you may abound in hope through the power of the Holy Ghost. (Romans 15:13 KJV)

CONTENTS

Introduction vii
Chapter 1: The Foundation 1
Chapter 2: A Struggling Country 7
Chapter 3: The House That Father Built 9
Chapter 4: Two-Room Schoolhouse 21
Chapter 5: Pathway to Destruction 25
Chapter 6: The Big City 29
Chapter 7: Path of Poverty 32
Chapter 8: Family Path 37
Chapter 9: Smelling the Coffee 45
Chapter 10: Heartbreak and Trouble 48
Chapter 11: Death Knocked Again 55
Chapter 12: Overcoming Obstacles 63
Chapter 13: Fire in the Cubicle 70
Chapter 14: A Service of Love 77
Chapter 15: Resilience and Determination 93
Chapter 16: Number 9—War Times 103
Chapter 17: Wishes Fly with the Wind 123
Acknowledgments 131

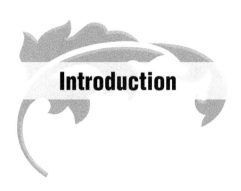

Introduction

In a dream, fifteen years ago, I awakened, saying, "Don't forget, just ask grandma." Throughout the years, I pondered, *Why should I remember such a strange statement? What could it mean?* When you finish this book, I hope that you will understand the statement's importance, as I have come to resolve the why.

My name is Thelma Flynn. I was born in 1946 in a family of ten children, living in the isolated Appalachian Mountains of Virginia—a family deep in poverty, with little education, day-to-day struggles, and many tragedies. There were many pitfalls this family faced living in poverty. They survived through their struggles year after year. Would backbreaking work get them back on top, or would it bury them? Sometimes they, and maybe you, are so low and so discouraged that you feel you need to reach up to touch the bottom. I am hopeful you find the strength to overcome any challenges that you may be facing. You will read about each child and their challenges, successes, and in some cases overcoming impossible odds.

My eldest sister, Shirley, lived a very tumultuous and complex life and chose to be estranged from the family for eighteen years. After a telephone call to her, it broke the chain that had her bound, and it opened the door so she could communicate with us again. I then was plunged deep into a life that was broken, battered, destroyed, and left empty, and a person who was crying for help from her sister.

As time passed, week after week I began receiving minitapes that my sister would dictate stories of unbelievable tales. Each week, she called, and we would talk about many things, including politics, which she loved. She would always say, "I am not proud of what I have done and don't listen to any tape until my death, then you can write a story." I kept that promise I made to her. As I have listened to some of the tapes, I feel her pain through her voice. She hurt so many with her actions, and yet she helped hundreds, maybe thousands, with her generosity, love, and compassion. However, people never knew who she was.

As a family of ten children, we were taught to love one another, forgive one another, and pray for one another. Nine of us chose to welcome our sister back into the family. One brother could not understand how she could abandon us, then waltz right back into our lives and expect us to forget everything.

Often we equate what is happening in life as just life. Yes, there is truth in that, however, we often find ourselves in situations that lead us down uncomfortable pathways, like my sister Shirley. This book does not capture many of the successes of this family. I will be focusing on the challenges these members faced, what poverty can do for you and against you, and how faith, hard work, and a good attitude will bring you out. I am prayerful and hoping that on some page of this book, you will find your strength and your reason for living. You are loved by many, including many strangers that you have not even met. We are all created in his image, loved by him, and loved by thousands who follow him.

There are many sources of information today. News cycles around the clock, social media platforms are endless, video, live stream, all the messages, so-called experts want you to hear and believe. Often the message is for you to believe and not question the information. It's their perspective, and often it is driven by the message to make money. Yes, I am hopeful about the financial success of this book, however, if one person finds their way in this life and serves their God, the time, and money spent on this project, then I will deem this a success!

In your life, you will have trouble, and you will have success. Every generation has its stories, and this generation will have its stories to tell. You can be a parent figure or grandparent figure to those that are strangers. Just getting involved is all it takes.

We look at Hollywood and the news media and see that money doesn't bring happiness. Yes, you are correct. We need money to survive and live a good life. Work hard to obtain all the things you want and deserve. However, it cannot be the only driving force. There are many examples where it has destroyed the greatest in their field of entertainment, science, technology, education, politics, and so on. Don't let your life be consumed with acquiring riches only. Riches will not satisfy the soul. Having peace, family, friends, and knowing your God, you will find it is most satisfying!

I am child number eight born in this family, and I don't know what it was like in the late 1930s and 1940s since I was born many years later. In some parts of this story, you may find it difficult to believe and understand. This is true as I was told by other family members, research, and my memory.

Chapter 1

The Foundation

As the electric and telephone lines weave from state to state, city to city, to large and small communities, rural to urban, over hills and down in the valleys, from the beginning of these pages to the very last word, ultimately the "lines of life run through the mountains" will be a message of hope to all that believe.

Recently, I realized stories of our American families are being lost. It appears families are not telling the younger generation their story. One reason could be so many families are broken by divorce. Children are shifted from one parent to another, and I believe history is being lost through the brokenness of the home.

There is a brokenness from divorce in many families, including my own children's lives. I decided I needed to tell our story so all future generations will know about our country, our families, challenges, successes, and how the people and country overcame unprecedented obstacles in the 1900s and beyond. Each year, families lose loved ones. Often we say, "I wish I had asked."

Being one of ten children born into a family living in the Appalachian Mountains of Virginia, we had many challenges, successes, and failures in the family of two hardworking parents—parents who knew and lived in a world of poverty. Yet there was a message of hope.

Garland, my father, was born in Laurel, Virginia, on June 10, 1908 or 1910. Records show conflicting dates. He passed away on February 14, 1988, from a stroke and pneumonia. Ruby Gladys, my mother, was born in Dorchester, Virginia, on November 23, 1910. She passed away from renal failure on January 29, 1987. Both Garland and Ruby are at rest in Cowpens, South Carolina.

When Ruby Gladys, my mother, met Garland, my father, in the hills of Virginia, they were struck with love. Garland's side of the family had one brother and two sisters. Gladys's side of the family had nine girls and one boy. Often families living in the community or next door married each other. This is the case in this family. The boys in Garland's family married sisters in Gladys's family. Garland and Gladys were married on January 17, 1931. For the next twenty years, they had children almost every two years until they reached child number ten.

Gladys was a short woman, about four feet, eleven inches tall, and weighed about ninety to one hundred pounds most of her life. Garland was not exceptionally tall, even though he always appeared tall since he was so thin. It was said he was about five feet, eleven inches, and about 140 pounds in his early life. He dressed in his one and only tailored three-piece suit and his wide-brim, almost velvety-feeling Stetson hat, and his accessory was a gold pocket watch.

In the thirties and forties, men and women did not go into public without the proper clothing, and Garland and Gladys were no exception. Garland would walk tall in his tailored suit, with his small, petite wife, Gladys, on his arm. Gladys often wore her only good dress, as she would call it. It was her Sunday go-to-meeting dress.

Gladys had one pair of dress shoes for her tiny feet. She was required to special order her shoes since a lady size two and a half wasn't stocked in the company store. Gladys often would stuff tissue paper in the toe of her shoes to help fill them out since they were often too large. If she didn't have the money to order the shoes, she would wear children's shoes that she could purchase at the local company store.

Employees worked for the local mines, and the mines owned the town. Employees and their families shopped at the company store. Employers paid their employees in script. The script was the company money and could only be spent at the company store. They had the system fixed for the company only, not the employees. Father was paid $1 a day and worked from sunrise until sunset; my oldest brother said.

Along with Garland and Gladys dressing properly in public, they tried to do the same with the children on Sunday. She dressed the family at their very best and attended church on Sunday.

In the summer, Gladys and the children would go barefoot to save wear and tear on the shoes, in hopes the shoes would be good to wear in the winter months. Each year, the girls got the same shoes: black and white Oxford. The girls hated those shoes. It seemed they would never wear out. That was the reason Gladys purchased those particular shoes. The girls would kick their toes and drag their feet so they would wear out. Gladys would cover the scuffs with white shoe polish or polish them up with her homemade biscuits. The lard in the biscuit made the shoes shine.

The six boys just seemed to wear anything they had or could get; it seemed to be acceptable with Gladys and society. However, society demanded much more from girls in those days. The girls could only dress in dresses. No slacks were ever allowed in our home for the girls. The words still echo: "What will the neighbors think?" Each member of the family needed to meet the expectations of the neighbors. Society and neighbors expected much from the girls. Poor behavior and poor manners would not be tolerated. If you were not spoken to, no need for you to just talk. Wait until you were asked for your opinion if you were ever asked. Times were different in those days.

Shirley Mae was the third born into this Appalachian family (February 5, 1936). She was sandwiched between two boys, Elvin Handy (January 20, 1932) and Robert Elbert (December 9, 1933), and two younger boys Charles Hubert (July 9, 1938) and Lee Eddie (January 18, 1941).

She had lots of opportunities to be picked on and blamed for everything that went wrong. Could it be that this type of childhood led this third-born child, Shirley, down the path of destruction and the path of success at the same time? Was it fate? Were others responsible for success and failure? How the questions seem to consume my thoughts. Did society play the most important role in the success or failure of another beautiful human being? The following pages may answer this question.

Just as today, we have experienced our country's struggle relating to the 2019 COVID pandemic, worldwide shutdown, loss of jobs, companies closing, poverty hitting all walks of life, stock market down, unemployment high, people locked down in their houses by our government. The government closed churches, businesses, gyms, and schools. Every human being, including infants, wears face coverings. Families are not allowed to visit their loved ones in hospitals and nursing homes. The government limited how many people could come to your home. The government required each person to stay six feet apart, and many other rules were listed on the government website.

Mandatory vaccination of medicine had very few trials conducted. Just take it and shut up was the thought! If you did not obey, you were at risk of going to jail or losing your job. You were an outcast and a person who was spreading misinformation if you disagreed with the medical community and government officials.

Yes, it is true. During 2020–2022, trouble was on every hand and everywhere you looked. Many people lost their jobs, homes, and bank accounts. Loneliness and suicide escalated due to isolation. The daily newscast was telling us what to do. Some agreed with getting vaccinated, and some disagreed.

Many people were in food lines week after week. Homelessness sored during the pandemic and beyond. The world is different after September 11, 2001, with the bombing of the World Trade buildings in New York, the Pentagon in Washington DC, and Flight 93 going down outside Shanksville, Pennsylvania. Oh, America, how far we have fallen. When will we awaken from these terrible and tragic times?

How did the people in the Appalachian mountain area fare during these difficult times in the 1930s and during 2020? A few years ago, I visited the area, and it was sad. Stores everywhere are closed. Buildings are in dire need of repair. Low-paying jobs and many people are out of work. There is little work there. Even Walmart closed and moved out of the area! It reminds me of what I have been told of the 1930s through 1940s. Poverty is everywhere you look.

Virginia is a very prosperous state, and yet the southwestern part of Virginia appears to be forgotten. These people are human beings who work hard, support the country, and serve in our military. These are proud and patriotic people, and many have given their lives for their country. In the center of the town of Appalachia, there is a memorial wall that lists members who have served in the Korean War. One member of this family is listed on that wall.

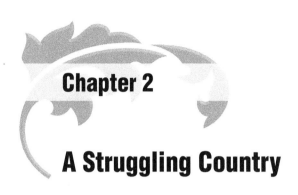

Chapter 2

A Struggling Country

We can be overcomers, no matter how difficult the situation appears. We often can see ourselves in the mirror of the lives of others through places, experiences, failures, and successes.

See how the roots of two poor hardworking people survived during the difficult times of the country, enduring poverty, and no work in rural America, and yet these parents raised a large family and survived its never-ending challenges.

I was told by siblings and parents that before their passing, getting a job, keeping a job, and providing for a family was almost impossible. The community as a whole was struggling to provide for their families, shoes on their feet, and clothes on the backs of their children. This was no exception for a family of ten children, surviving on a nonunion miner's pay. It was surviving from dawn, the coming up of the sun, to dusk, the setting at the end of that day.

Children were always hungry, and parents were always tired and weary from the hard day of work in the coal mine and in the field. Day in and day out, year in and year out seemed to always be the same: poverty! This journey is hard for many to understand. Their finances, education, and part of the country they lived in may have been more prosperous than in the coal fields. There is a great difference between prosperous and poverty areas of the country. Many were and are still living in extreme poverty in Appalachia.

As history tells us, our country was going through very challenging times, which extended to families across the nation. During the 1920s, the US economy expanded rapidly, and the nation's wealth more than doubled. There was prosperity in the country. The nation referred to this time in the country as "the Roaring Twenties". Did America get too comfortable during these times?

Yes, wealthy Americans enjoyed the rapid stock market increase until that fatal day, October 29, 1929. The stock market crashed, wiping out billions of dollars. However, even with the loss of billions, some Americans increased their wealth.

Most working-class people had no money in the stock market. It was a time when the rich got richer and the poor became poorer. My parents said times were hard under the presidency of Herbert Hoover.

President Hoover lost the presidency in 1932 to Franklin D. Roosevelt. The country faced World War II from 1939 until 1945. World War II ended with the Japanese surrender in September 1945. The stock market crash of 1929, and through the years of the war, the whole world felt the impact.

When you are poor or lower middle class, you know the real challenges, struggles, failures, and successes because you live them daily.

During this time, people worried about how to feed their families and keep a roof over their heads. How to put clothes on the backs of their children. Thousands of people asked these questions.

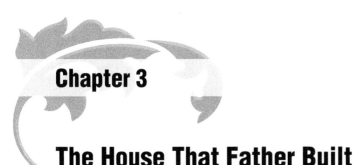

Chapter 3

The House That Father Built

In the late 1930s, my brother said they lived in a house that was built with wood slabs. It must not have been secure, since when a windstorm came up, the house blew over the hill. He remembers staying with his aunts, and building began again.

Deep in the holler of Virginia, there was a big wooden house that Garland and his cousin Elmer helped build. They did not own this house. They never owned a home until late in their life. As I was told, Father said land was $0.50 an acre, and a large new home was about $800. Yet he owned no land and no home. He said that he didn't have $0.50 to purchase land and build a home, so they had no choice but to rent.

The firstborn, my eldest brother, Elvin, remembers, at least three of the ten children were born in this house. He said, there were a few other houses around in that area as well. We were not the only neighbors in that holler. He remembers the building of this house.

Elvin remembers he broke his leg while the house was being built. In those days, a person breaking a bone or becoming ill set a huge burden on the family. There was no health insurance, and the cost of going to a doctor or the doctor coming to the house placed such a burden on the coal miner's family. The children did not understand this, nor should they. Children don't need to know the challenges of the parents raising them. They will face these challenges with their own families not many years in the future.

I was told, "We just couldn't help ourselves from climbing up the apple tree or jumping off the huge boulders that encamped the area, and then you found yourself screaming for help after you fell and hurt yourself." If you got hurt, in most cases, you got a bottle of rubbing alcohol poured onto the injury and wrapped it. Gladys and Garland would pray that you got better.

Gladys was the family doctor and could cure almost any illness the ten children encountered. Home remedies and stories of "cures" passed down from previous generations and other members in the "camp" were practices tried and true, no matter how ridiculous they seemed to be. For example, my father would blow cigarette smoke into the ear for an earache. Father would take urine from the person who had an earache and place two or three drops into the ear. Once a week, Mother would give each child a spoon of castor oil to keep the body cleansed.

Behind this house in the holler was a swing, and the eldest girl, child number three, Shirley, wanted to swing there every day. However, that area was forbidden by Gladys since there was a coal mine there, and all of the sawdust from previous sawmills made the area soft and very dangerous. You could step in the sawdust and be buried instantly.

As a child, she knew no danger, and of course, she disobeyed Gladys. She figured, since there were no toys, no bicycle, no swing, only a Chinese checker game and plenty of rocks in the yard to play with, what would it hurt if she would swing a little while?

At a young age, she did not realize the community watched out for each other's children. The lady who lived close to the bridge and the swing was always keeping an eye out for any wrongdoings of the children who wanted to go to that swing. As I remember, Shirley told me, "I just could not help myself. The swing kept calling me to 'come swing today.'" She said, "I obeyed the swing, and I went across the bridge. And that little old lady told Gladys that she saw me swinging, and Gladys whipped me that very night. From that night on, I began to hate." Hate began filling her heart for people who were mean to her, and she had made up her mind that if people were mean to her, she would get even. She said, to this day, she believes she cast a spell on that old woman. She said that she truly hated that woman for telling on her and getting her in trouble.

Shirley said that she had been taught to be kind to people, so she got the idea: "If I gave that old lady apples, she wouldn't tell on me when I go back to the swing." So she gathered up red apples and polished them until they were just right and then took them to the old lady. She remembered how pleased the old lady was to get the apples. Shirley didn't do it to make her feel good; Shirley just wanted the old lady to keep her mouth shut and not get her in trouble.

Shirley didn't realize that when she went to swing, her favorite blue velvet dress along with her shoes would be dirty, and they would tell on her when Gladys saw her. She said, "I had such a good time swinging and letting the wind hit my face." Gladys knew, without getting word from the neighbor, what she had done. But as a child, she just knew the old lady told on her again, and that is when she killed her! Yes, that is right. "I killed her that very night," Shirley said. She did not kill her with a weapon or do damage to her house; Shirley was convinced that she did kill her.

That very night, a neighbor came running to our house asking Gladys to come to help the little old lady who was sick. Gladys took off running to the little old lady's house. Shirley just smiled on the inside because she knew she was dead or would be dead shortly. And sure enough, at the stroke of midnight, she died. She said, "I was so, so happy, but I could not let Mother know that I did not feel any remorse for that old lady."

Shirley was glad she was gone. Right there and then, Shirley knew that from now on, she could get rid of anyone who hurt her again. I asked, "Why do you feel responsible for her death? You were only a child. There is no way you caused her death," and she just said, "Well, I know the difference." So I asked if she would tell me how she did this terrible thing, and she replied, "Later." Over time, she expressed how she killed a lady when she was just a child and got away with it. Shirley said she knew, in scary stories, bad things happened at midnight. She just had to wish for it at the right time of the night and the right day, when she was really angry.

Time went by, and time passed on until that fatal night. She remembers it being a little cool that evening. That night, darkness was quickly approaching, and she wanted to be sure no one would stop her exciting plan. She did not want anyone around who could help the old lady escape her curse. Once the old lady's breathing stopped and the heart no longer worked, she would be free from her and free as the birds that flew around all day. Shirley said, "The birds have it made. They don't have to work. They don't have to listen to someone telling them what to do, not even God. God just gives them everything they need to live, and he just sits back and enjoys them."

She thought she was going to be that free too, and there would be no one again telling her mother anything about her.

To this day, child three, Shirley, speaks of never wishing death on anyone because she thought she had the power to make it happen. Could she cause death to someone by just making a death wish? Is this possible? How can we prove if it is true or prove it is untrue?

As Shirley got older, the family moved again, this time not quite as far back into the holler as the other old house. This time, they lived right in a curve at the bottom of a mountain, close to the state line, heading into Kentucky. I was told times were harder than ever for the family. While living in this house, my brother Hubert was hit by a car and broke several bones, so our brother Lee picked up his chores until he got better. The family had no insurance to pay the hospital bill; however, most people in those days did the right thing and paid their obligations. The person who hit him with the car paid the hospital bill.

Shirley said, "Father would work all week and was away from home again and again since he had no way to get back home. He would sleep in the coal mines until he could catch a ride home on Friday."

All of the hard work of the land and home maintenance was placed on the boys, and housework was placed on the mother and the girls. Washing of the clothes was done by hand on a scrub board in a large galvanized tub. Dishes were done by hand, and water was carried to wash them, washing dishes in one pan and then rinsing them in another pan. Gladys would throw the water out and get fresh water in between washing. The girls hated to throw out the water while washing dishes when they were not even finished that just meant they had to go get more water. Ironing was done with irons heated on the wood stove. The one hundred pounds block of ice was placed in the ice box refrigerator each week.

Preserving the food was also hard. A fire was built in the yard over a galvanized tube. We would carry water and wash the jars. Then the jars were placed in a tub of hot water to sterilize them. After sterilizing the jars and lids in one tub, Mother would fill the jars with food and place those jars into the second galvanized tub of water, and everyone worked to keep the fire hot for hours while the tub of food was being processed. Mother canned everything we grew and any fruit we picked from all of the fruit trees and berry bushes. As winter deepened, spring and early summer approached. The canned food was gone, and food in our home became scarce.

As children, we learned to preserve food since it was a skill that we must have to survive in the world, Mother said.

The water hole was used as the bathhouse, swimming hole, and place of drinking water. All of the children would carry water to the house several times a day. You see, there was no running water in the house. Dishwashers had not been invented, at least in this house. I was told, "We knew nothing about modern appliances if there were any."

There was no indoor bathroom, no phone, no cell phone, and no television, only one large standing radio that the family gathered around for the nightly stories from the people inside the radio. *Fibber McGee and Molly* was one story! The radio sat next to a potbellied stove and a fireplace, where we roasted potatoes at night and peeled apples by the night fire. I asked my siblings, and no one in the family remembers having lights in this house, so that meant shortly after dark, everyone went to bed.

My memory takes me back to the old mountain place of my childhood with my parents and siblings. The area I see is pristine in its appearance, with lush native grasses, tall trees, and endless blue skies which bring a flurry of emotions. I recall standing on the front porch, where you could see a field of fruit trees, berry bushes, thorns, and thistles. From the porch, you could see the tree with the car tire tied to a strong rope, which Father prepared as a swing for the children to enjoy.

Looking in the other direction was a lonely dusty road, and going straight would lead you to water flowing down a small waterfall, and over big, flat, water-smooth rocks and under them was the place where cold items, such as watermelons and cantaloupes, and Father would hide his moonshine. Of course, he thought it was well hidden from the children—not so. They knew exactly where he hid his moonshine.

Looking outside, it was pitch black, and you could hear the coyotes howling, owls hooting, crickets chirping, and water running over the waterfalls, and often in the distance, the sound of thunder and buckets of water raining from the sky from the angel's tears, as Mother would say. There were times when the morning sun would come up, and the boys would go feed the chickens. They would return with stories that "something got into the chicken house last night." As a poor family, chickens and the eggs that they laid were an important part of our life. The family could not afford for the animals to return again and again. The boys watched with their twenty-gauge shotgun night after night until they killed the beast that attacked their livelihood.

Father often spoke of some kind of animal that the community was afraid of, and it was always the talk of the town. He said they could hear it making sounds in the night, and no one ever saw or caught that animal. I wonder if it was Bigfoot.

In front of this old washed-out, broken-down, white house was a huge rock. The rock was located on top of a hill, overlooking the highway in a curve, heading up another mountain going into Kentucky. This rock or boulder held many secrets from a family of ten. As I was told, "As we sat on that huge rock, many of us told secrets to the rock. The rock never told our secrets. We even carved our names into the rock as we became old enough to do so." The names are still there today, but some of the names have faded because of the weather.

Shirley said, "There were stories told to the rock, and dreams were made on that rock. And we did many things on that rock that we are not proud of. One story was that the boys would take off their clothes and stand there on the rock and wave at the cars going by, and Father would say, they stood there as "naked as a jaybird."

Shirley dreamed of leaving the holler, getting a good job, a big house with store-bought sheets and a real mattress. She said, "I heard that mattress was made of soft material, but the one that I slept on was made of leaves." Each fall, Mother would empty the leaves of the mattresses and pillows, and we would pick up new leaves for all of them. If Mother had enough feathers, some pillows would be filled with feathers. Shirley dreamed big dreams and saw herself with beautiful clothes, pretty diamond rings, and hair so beautiful, and she could smell the perfume that she dreamed of just bathing in.

If you look at the house from the outside and pretend to draw two boxes, one to the left and one to the right, then with three steps going right up between the two boxes, that is the layout of the house. The porch was not screened in; it was all open. Walking into the house, to the right was a bedroom, and to your right was a little closet with a window overlooking the road. This is the room Mother used when she prayed. I recall her praying often for two boys who went into the military and for her husband who was working in the coal mines. Past the kitchen was another bedroom. In their younger life, the girls and boys slept together in the same room.

We had no curtains or blinds at any of the windows. Father didn't believe in window treatment of any kind. He believed the windows were made to let light in, and you to look out.

Shirley said, she recalls how she felt when she got anything new. Even if Mother made it, she felt it was like a million dollars, of course not having any clue how much a million dollars was.

I remember sitting on boxes and eating apples as Mother would peel them at night when they were in season, or we would get them from the cellar where Father stored them in the fall, and we would have fruit all winter.

The best part of the house was the big, white back porch with lots of steps, and I recall the back bedroom of the house had two windows, where you could look out over Father's twelve white beehives that had belonged to his brother, Corbin, who passed away in 1946. The hives sat on a mountain of sawdust. You could fall into those deep, deep pits and be swallowed up by the sawdust piles, yet we played there every day, year in and year out. I suppose we were always watched over by the Lord above. As my siblings and I look back, it was truly a miracle that no one was hurt or bitten by a snake while playing in the dust piles. Oh, how dangerous that was!

When the honey was removed from the beehives, for the extra money, it was sold on the public road for $1 a quart, along with berries and vegetables from our garden. Father would have the boys go to the railroad tracks. And when the train would pass, often pieces of coal would fall off the train cars. The boys would collect the pieces of coal, place them in bags, and sell them on the side of the road for $0.10 a bag. Father would also trap wildlife and fish and hunt animals that were in season, which also provided food for the family. When Father had a pig or could get a pigskin from a neighbor, he would scrap the fat, and Mother would make soap. She would render lard for cooking from the skin. Pig feet were pickled, and the family would eat in the winter.

Father was not able to acquire a good-paying job if there was one to be found. You see, he had no formal education. The story was told he went to school only one day, and it was said he had to stand since there were not enough seats in the classroom for every student. When he returned home from the first day of class, his dad said, "You are not going back." And he didn't. Therefore, he never learned to read or write. All through life, anything that needed to be read, Mother would read it to him.

Over time, he learned to recognize his name when it was written. He would mark an X for his signature. Father was educated in the game of life. Father was extremely good with math and could tell you, within seconds, numbers and totals. You could not cheat Father—he watched the numbers!

Mother went to the third grade of school. She, with her great learning, was able to manage and budget the family finances. Mother would read to Father from the Bible each night, and he would ask her to explain what she read to him. For some reason, Mother had in-depth knowledge of the Scriptures. "I don't know how I know. I just know," She would say. That in itself was a miracle since Mother struggled to read and understand, even a recipe. Times were hard for families in the coal country. With so much manual labor, children were often kept home and not allowed to go to school.

We were satisfied with having only the bare necessities because we had each other. Shirley said, "I have four brothers to play with, and my mother was always having another child every two years for twenty years."

As spring approached, everyone worked in the garden, plowing with the old mule. Planting and sowing seeds and praying the seeds and plants would take root and grow. We had a huge field of berries. And as the berries came on the vines, we would pick them and sell them by the road for extra family income. I remember sitting in the field, eating berries, making mud cakes, drying them in the sun, and eating them like they were candy.

There were snakes on the property, and poisonous ones at that! It is amazing that, to my knowledge, none of the children were ever bitten by the snakes. Since we lived a long way from the hospital and had no transportation available, the victim would probably have died from a snake bite. It is amazing how people can and do survive in the most distressed conditions. They can survive with little and flourish in times of plenty. Times were also hard for our community, and the nation was struggling.

Mother told a story about one potato. The firstborn child, Elvin, was about sixteen or seventeen years of age and, as all youth, always hungry. Mother said, "There is one large potato in the bin. You can eat it tonight, and there won't be any food until your father gets home tomorrow evening. Or you can wait until tomorrow, and I will fix it and make water gravy, and we all can eat." He chose to wait. Mother said it worried her all night thinking that if something happened to him that night, she would never forgive herself for not allowing him to eat the potato.

Little pleasures and little money only made them stronger and a very tight-knit family in their adult lives. This family is strong, healthy, hardworking, contributing to society, kind, good, and above all, God-fearing, as Mother taught us to be. Child number three strayed a while from the parents' teaching.

It is truly a mystery and an unbelievable story as to how this mountain family survived during the time the country was struggling to survive too. It was a miracle. With God's help and a little countrywoman called Mother, we survived unbelievable poverty, and the children grew up and became successful.

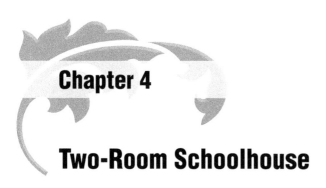

Chapter 4

Two-Room Schoolhouse

Merriam-Webster says an Appalachian is a native or resident of the Appalachian mountain area. I am an Appalachian.

Living in the city during my adolescent and teenage years, I was ashamed of my mountain roots. The stereotype in Baltimore for people from Virginia was so negative and hurtful that I tried to distance myself from my heritage. I was determined to prove I was not one of the people they knew and laughed about. I listened to how others spoke words and the dialect and tried to emulate them. I worked hard to get rid of my Southern accent, and for many years, when asked where I was from, I would say Baltimore.

The schools in Baltimore were tall buildings with several floors, playgrounds, and fences around them so children could run and play and not get hit by a car. In Virginia, from the first to third grade I attended, it was a two-room schoolhouse. There was a bridge across the little stream of water, which I think was Looney Creek. My teacher would come out on that bridge in her long full-cotton dress with an apron over the top, her hair gathered on top of her head, and she would go to the center of the bridge and begin ringing the bell.

The bell had a handle about six or eight inches long, and the bell casing was attached to the handle. The ringing of a bell is a unique sound that you don't hear much today. *Ding dong, ding dong*, and all the children came running to the sound of the bell.

In the classroom was a large potbellied stove, where Mrs. Palmer would feed the stove all day with coal and pieces of wood. On top of the stove, she would heat corn beef in a pot. Mother said canned corn beef and blocks of cheese came from the state to help feed the children. Mrs. Palmer would make us sandwiches at noon each day. She always had a stash of candy bars that you could purchase from her if you had money. Now that I am older, I bet she gave more candy bars away than she sold.

The student's desks were the old-fashion wooded desks with a hole in the right side of the desktop where you would place the little bottle of ink, which you would place the ink pin in and suck up the ink into the pen to write with. Under the desktop was an opening where you placed your books or other personal items. The desk was in rows, and, yes, the boys would indeed sit behind you and pull the girl's hair!

The front of the room had lots of chalkboards. Above the chalkboards were all of the alphabet letters, small and capital letters. You practiced writing the letters like the letters on the wall. Mrs. Palmer would walk around the room and ensure you were writing correctly. You were going to have good penmanship, listen, and obey her commands, or else.

You see, in those days, the teachers could spank you, and spank you she did if she felt you deserved a spanking. Parents did not get angry at the teacher if they were spanked. If you got a spanking in school, you got a spanking when you got home too. I do recall my sister Shirley saying she was spanked. Most likely, my brother Larry received a school spanking. He took one of the large tomcats and placed it in the coatroom, and the cat destroyed the coatroom and all that was in it. He remembers he was corrected, and he never pulled that stunt again. I don't believe I was ever spanked in school, or it could be a memory that I have chosen to forget.

When you passed from the second grade, you would go around the corner to the third-grade class. It too was set up just like the other classroom.

There was no air conditioning in those days in homes, stores, or schools. Yes, we went to school when it was hot, and we did not get to go home early because it was too hot in the classroom. The teacher would open the windows, and you finished your day of school, hot or not. Not only was there no air conditioning, there were no indoor bathrooms and no sinks to get a drink of water. The bathroom was an outhouse that you could visit if you were permitted by raising your hand, and the teacher would acknowledge you. The toilet tissue was usually a Sears and Roebucks or Montgomery Ward catalog. What page of the catalog were we going to use today?

If you wanted a drink, Mrs. Palmer would draw a dipper of water from the pail and place it in a glass for you. I assume she would draw water from the well before we arrived at school.

It was fun when Mrs. Palmer allowed the students to write on the chalkboard, clean the erasers, and wash the boards for her.

Once you passed the third grade, you would go to Appalachia High School. I attended the high school for a few months before we moved to Maryland. Neither of the two old schoolhouses exists now; they have been replaced and are located on other sites. There are only memories of the little two-room schoolhouse and the high school that seemed so large and intimidating to a shy fourth grader.

Near the high school was a restaurant, where sometimes we could go to purchase our lunch. You see, Father had a "tab" there, as it was called. We would order a hot dog or sandwich and say, "Put it on daddy's tab." I guess everyone knew everyone in the small town.

I remember kneeling in front of the porch swing with my schoolbooks on the seat, attempting to do my homework. I recall one particular time, when I was struggling to understand what to do. I began to cry, and my mother said, "I don't know how to help you." I got no mercy, and the answer was, "You must figure it out." I suppose I figured it out, and this is what you do your entire life: Don't quit—you can do it, figure it out!

I was told there was a skating rink, a movie theater, and several diners in our little town, and one hotel had an outside swimming pool. Most of our swimming was done in the creek. There is a historical, unique building in Appalachia that is worth mentioning in this book. The building is a four-story building, and each floor exits onto the sidewalk. You first say, how could that be? You see, it is located on the hill, and each of the entrances comes out on each level of the hill. As a child, this building was often pointed out to the children as something special for us to see and remember. As children, we don't remember doing anything outside of working in Virginia. My sister Shirley remembers going skating one time with a friend when she was about fifteen, and she wore pants. Father found out and came to the skating rink, spanked her, and forbade her to ever go there again.

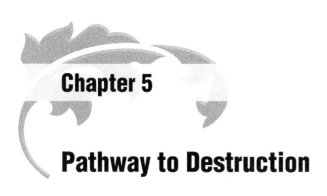

Chapter 5

Pathway to Destruction

As I think of the paths that families often take, it saddens me. I ponder how a child who seems to have it all together walks down the road, leading to destruction, and doesn't see the warning signs blinking. "Don't do that, trouble lies ahead." For some reason, the forces seem to persuade the person to go down the path of destruction, even when they feel deep within their gut that there is something wrong with the decision they are about to make. Every person who finds themselves in this place must find the strength to say *stop* or *no*, and when you do, it will change your life forever. God has built into our lives a system that helps us; it's called that gut feeling. It is a still, small voice of a higher power.

In your lifetime, that fork in the road will come, and you will make decisions that will define your future. One road will have a gravitational pull to the left, and that road is always paved with good intentions. Those intentions often become so cloudy and dark that a ray of light cannot break through to free you from the darkness of a broken and tangled web that has captured your being.

You can see the other side, the right side of the road, the road to success and freedom, but you can't get there. You are empty crying for help, but the words won't come out of your mouth. In the heart, soul, and gut, you say, "There must be a better way, and this just cannot be my destiny." You will think those thoughts, ponder them in your heart and soul, and want to be a better person. You pound your head against the wall and not just in your mind. You will beat on the floor on your bended knees. You will shout to the trees and forest and yet feel no words echoing back to you. You are correct. Most of the time, when you are in the darkest place in life or the most confused state of despair, you have lost all hope; you may have lost your family, and there is no one to reach out to. You never dreamed you would be in this place. You will say, "I am a poor and broken individual." This is where the road to the left may have taken you.

When you look back at that fork in the road to the right, what did you see? You didn't want that road, even though there was much beauty there. It just didn't look like it was a place to have fun and express yourself. It looked boring.

You may say, "I wish I could go back to my days of innocence." You know that is only a dream. We can't erase the past, but we need to improve our future and change what we can change. We must accept what we cannot change. We must find the strength to go on. Hard times will either make you better or make you bitter.

I see beautiful flowers that line both sides of the road. I can see the most beautiful tree reaching high into the sky, birds on branches singing such beautiful songs. I see a farmer and his family in the field, digging and hoeing their vegetable garden. The woman has a large, white hat, trimmed in black. It reminds me of a hat that I used to wear in the garden, and my grandson at the age of ten loved that

hat. He would put it on and get on the gravely lawn mower, and off he would go. You can see him in the field with the hat just flopping in the wind. The farmer's hat is camouflaged with pull strings that would tighten around his chin. He's bending over and standing up, hoeing, pulling those weeds that are choking out his vegetables. The weeds want to choke the life right out of his soon-to-be crop. The farmer was going at those weeds with vengeance. The farmer is aware if he does not get those weeds under control. They will take over that whole garden, then no crop to feed his family.

Just as this garden correlates with the fork in the road, you must get the outcome you are striving for. Then you ask, "How do I do that?" It is not easy; however, it is obtainable. You continue to fight. Don't quit when times get tough, and don't give up when you can't understand the circumstances you are in. Keep working until you succeed.

Remember, life is like a candle, and one day, the candle of life will go out. Life is short, even when you live to an old age. Will the light of life go out quickly, or will the light of life linger on year after year in some unhealthy situation? That is unknown. Only time will tell.

If you have taken the road to the left as my sister Shirley did, by now you find yourself with several children, no father or mother to them, no husband, no wife, and you may have a disease. You may have habits consuming your finances. You can't find a job. You have a drug record, and you've been arrested too many times. Poor credit. When a potential employer checks your credit, he will not hire you; he can't trust you. You are locked in a world of poverty. This force pulls and tugs at you from the time you were very young. You are sure your parents were old-fashioned and didn't know a thing when they tried to lead you to a better life.

As you go through life, you are constantly full of questions. We often say, "Should I do this?" or "Should I do that?" or "Please someone tell me what to do. What career should I pursue? What college should I attend? Who should I marry? Where should I live? Should I have children? Should I not have children?" We struggle to find the correct answers. Then one day, we realize we have aged.

We look back. What did I do with all the years God gave me? Who did I help? Where are the things I spend my money on? Yes, I made the right choice. No, I made terrible choices. No matter what your successes are, usually it's never enough to satisfy you.

The good book says, "The eyes of man are never satisfied." Just as successes, your failures are usually not as bad as you think. It is obvious; you survived. Let us not allow our life successes or failures to torment, rob, kill, or destroy the rest of our lives. Do not allow them to destroy another generation of family and friends. You are a surviving family, surviving individuals, and surviving community, and we are a surviving nation.

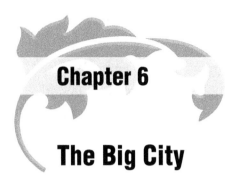

Chapter 6

The Big City

There are two paths in life that one can choose. My sister Shirley took the road to the left, and I, Thelma, took the road to the right—two very opposite lives. I chose to serve the Lord, and Shirley served the world.

When we are on the interstate of life, we keep going around and around unless there is an exit to get off. My sister lived on that interstate most of her life, searching for that exit.

Through my eyes, I see how your past will continue to drive your future, good or bad. You must face your future head-on. Pain and hurt will not go away unless we admit to our successes and our failures and receive healing for the things that we could not or did not change. Our lives are full of stories of struggle and often disappointment; however, it is also full of hope and success.

Our lives are like this manuscript. I captured my thoughts with pen, paper, and computer. I have written and discarded page after page and did a rewrite over and over again, trying to capture what I believe will help you as you read each story. Life is like that. We work at improving ourselves every day. Some days, we like what we have become; other days, we are disappointed with life and ourselves.

Many can relate to these words. We are all God's creation and have the same challenges throughout life. You see, we all have scars from our past. The scars will always be there, but they fade and become less noticeable as life goes on. Scars never completely go away. We are taught to forgive, and sometimes we can, but other times, it is harder to do. Although we work to find the strength to forgive, our minds won't allow us to forget.

Shirley said, "Sometimes I wish I could go back to the simple life, living in the Appalachian Mountains of Virginia, and there I could wash away the pain and hurt that I experienced while living the city life. Then I think, would I still love the city, all that it offered, all that it gave, including the pain and hurt? And the answer is yes."

In our little town, Inman, Virginia, there was a one-room post office and a country store. The steps of the country store were the meeting place for the men of the community. I recall my father, Garland, and the other men sitting on the front steps, having their pocket knives in hand. They were ready to whittle on the stick they picked up on the way to their gathering place. On these steps, many problems, issues, and deals were made. No paper contract, just a shake of the hand sealed every deal.

These men seemed content with country living. They had no idea what the big city job market could provide for them. The city possibly could provide a much better living for their families.

Why did they like this place? It seemed they were stuck in a rut. Why would they not leave this place, if not for their self-worth, for the family's sake? Why would they want to stay in a place and struggle? My sister said, "I will not be like them. I will leave this place and never return. I am going to have all the things that money can buy. I am going to be rich, famous, and dress in the finest clothes."

One day, Shirley arrived in the city of Baltimore. "Look at this place. Everyone must be rich and so happy here. I can't wait to begin this new journey." The city was amazing. The beautiful big buildings and lights shining against the night sky hid the stars that she saw so clearly while living in the country. This was the most beautiful place that she had ever seen. She thought, *I will live here forever. I don't miss the country at all. I feel like I am finally free from the country living.*

She said she would not allow the city nightlife and all its corruption to tempt and tease her. She said she was stronger and smarter than any other person her age. If she decided to taste everything the city has to offer, she could control it. She said, "I am sure it was going to be a wonderful experience," and she looked forward to her new travels.

Chapter 7

Path of Poverty

One way out of poverty, when you had such a large family, was to encourage the children to get a life of their own as soon as possible. We were told, "When you reach the age of eighteen, you either marry or get a place of your own, and you will move out and be on your own." This is what society encouraged too. If you were beyond eighteen and not married, you were often named "an old maid." We were told by our parents that when you marry, select well. There is no divorce! We were not encouraged to stay in school. Girls were to take care of the home and have children; the boys were expected to work and take care of their families. If you quit school or you chose to graduate, mothers would say, "You will meet someone. You marry them. And that's it." That's what we were told. And as each child turned eighteen (or less), we did just that: move out of our parents' home and start our own life.

The older boys, Elvin and Robert, quit school. The law required them to register to be drafted into the military. The two boys were now in the army. When the boys went off to serve our country, one was stationed at Fort Bragg, North Carolina, and the other went to

Korea. My eldest brother, Elvin, served in Korea. He did not want to leave the States. And my brother Robert was stationed stateside. He wanted to go overseas. The very opposite happened. Robert, who was stationed stateside, met his beautiful bride and his lifetime partner in North Carolina. Elvin was assigned to Korea. He told about the day the soldiers left the United States and arrived at their destination: Korea. They could hear the firing of the guns. "It was an eerie feeling," he recalled. He remembers leaving his humble home and traveling around the world to fight and defend our country, the USA. He recalled the day they arrived by ship at their final destination, Korea. He also recalled that a peace treaty was signed the day his troops arrived in Korea. There was no actual peace treaty signed, but the men stopped shooting at each other. He was there for a while but not firing at the man on the opposite side of the military action, the Koreans.

When Elvin, child number 1, was getting near the end of his military service, it was around 1954. Robert, child number two, entered the army. They were two years apart in age.

Men in Korea remained there for some time, cleaning up from the war. The boys were young and didn't understand why they were fighting. They just did as they were ordered to do.

The country was told by our leaders, "The US initially didn't want to get involved in any kind of invasion. They didn't want to get tangled up with North Korea, much less with China or the Soviet Union." In August 1949, the Soviets detonated their first atomic bomb. A physicist who helped the United States build its bomb program leaked the blueprint of the Fat Man bomb. The revelations stoked Cold War fears among us and the Soviet Union.

On April 14, 1950, Truman received the National Security Council Paper, created by the defense department, the state department, the CIA, and other agencies. It advised the president to grow the defense industry to counter what agencies saw as threatening global communism growth. The recommendations cemented Truman's next move.

On June 27, 1950, President Truman ordered US forces to South Korea to repress the North's invasion. "Democrats needed to look tough on communism." Truman used Korea to send a message that the US would contain communism and come to the aid of their allies.

On December 16, 1950, US President Harry Truman declared a state of emergency, proclaiming that "communist imperialism" was a threat to democracy. The United States never formally declared war on North Korea. Instead, Truman referred to the addition of ground troops as a police action.

The Korean War armistice, signed on July 27, 1953, drew a new border between North Korea and South Korea, granting South Korea some additional territory and demilitarizing the zone between the two nations. A formal peace treaty was never signed.

Back home in Virginia, the family continued to struggle; however, the boys were sending money home to help Father raise the other children. Mother said it was a big help to the family. Elvin purchased Mother's first gas-engine washing machine when he returned from the Korean War.

Now that two older brothers were out of the house, and serving their country. Mother now was focused on Shirley. Shirley was maturing into a young woman, and that caused her mother to fear what would become of her. Mother said raising boys was easier than raising girls.

As Shirley grew into her teens, her mother had no money to buy her sanitary products or undergarments. Being a young girl, her breasts were growing, and her nipples would show through her clothes. Shirley indicated she was so embarrassed. Mother said, "Put tape over the nipples so they don't show." Shirley remembers that after she got married, her husband bought her very first bra. Can you believe that? Today we buy from the most expensive stores and toss those old clothes we bought months ago into the recycling bin at thrift stores. Do you know what it is like not to have any new or old clothes to place in a recycle bin?

Shirley indicated that our parents were so afraid she would get pregnant, and it would be such a hardship on the family to raise another child and a total disgrace to the family that they pushed her to marry a man who was much older than she was. Her first husband, Dayton, was a broken man himself. He was three years old when his father committed suicide, and it is said that his mother left him on the roadside since his mother could not care for him. It was said he was in foster care and taken in by another family. The foster family officially adopted him when he was twenty-one years of age, and he was getting ready to go into the army. His birth name was also changed to his new foster name. He was a hard worker who ran heavy road equipment and made "really good money," she said, however, had a dark disease: alcoholism.

At first, he was good to her and bought her nice things. She said she didn't know what love was at that time; she was just too young. She tried so hard to be a good wife and to meet his needs. When he drank, he was not nice. He was mean and broke things. She was so scared most of the time.

After getting married, eleven months and nine days later, they had their one and only child. As the years went by, her husband became more and more abusive. One time, she recalls, he was so drunk and came home and started shooting into the house. She said she then grabbed her son and hid behind the counter. His shots were so close that she believed only God protected them that night. After this incident, she filed for a divorce in Virginia in December 1956. This naive young country girl left a very poor home and entered an abuser's home.

From that incident on, she said, "I just wanted to get even with the men for hurting me." She believed she possessed such powers to hurt them. Were those thoughts from the devil? The devil became her leader and her friend. She said, "He told me to do something, and I did it." These thoughts and desires followed her for a large majority of her life and brought good and bad times to her life. She shared a thought that she lived by for many years "I had to be bad before I can become good." She had to be broken badly before she would change her way of living because she said, "I enjoyed the nightlife, and the green (money) that it brought me. I did not want to be a Christian or be good. I did not want God telling me what to do, yet the devil told me what to do every waking minute. He cracked the whip, and I jumped to his command."

Chapter 8

Family Path

As years went by, the local mines closed. Father lost his job, and he could not find work in Virginia. By this time, the older boys were out on their own and were in Maryland. The family packed up and off to Baltimore, Maryland, in 1956.

There we lived in a three-room apartment on the third floor until Father could find a job and get a larger place. What a change for the six children going from the wide-open space to a crowded place and three rooms. The younger children had never been in a house with stairs and got lost going to our apartment.

The children were perplexed that other people lived in the house too. It was very frightening when the children came down the stairs, and a man was sitting at the table on the second floor, and it wasn't our father. Could we stand to live in this house with different men and women? This was very strange to the six children still at home. This was a really strange place to live.

People were all over the place. And houses were all attached, and there were no trees and no grass but very tall buildings that the children had never seen before. Where would we play with no trees to climb, no stream to swim in, and no outside toilet? Wow, they placed a toilet and bathtub in a house; what an idea!

The people next door laughed at the way we spoke. They said all of us talked funny, and we thought that was strange because they were the ones who talked funny, not us. The young people were throwing balls up against the front of the brick houses and catching them. They were doing cartwheels right on the concrete sidewalks. There were no swings, nowhere to throw rocks, no place to push our bicycle wheel, with our coat rack handle over stones to see who could keep the wheel going. Instead, we were learning how to play a game that was foreign to us: hopscotch, shuffleboard, and dancing inside a building called the recreation center with music. And they had food in there too. Young people were running around with these metal taps on their shoes, boys with basketballs, boys lifting heavy weights—all such a new world to us.

We went to the store every day and purchased what Mother would prepare for dinner. Mother said this was the only way she could feed us. If food was in the house, we ate it up. The usual purchase was canned beans, canned corn, potatoes, and cornmeal to prepare cornbread and usually bacon for Father. We may get some apples or oranges so we can have a snack before bed. We worked hard, played hard, and ate light since food was scarce.

I remember Father working on a fruit wagon, and at the end of the day, they would often have leftover fruit that was going bad or didn't sell. But the man that he worked for would not give it to him; instead, he would put it in the trash. Father hated that man since the man knew our father had a large family and did not have much money. This man was our father's brother-in-law. He was married to Mother's sister. Father said he never had any respect for him after that. As soon as Father found another job, he left and never went back to work with his brother-in-law again. Needless to say, we were not close to this aunt, uncle, and cousins. Our father would not allow us to visit them. However, Mother did not feel the same way.

During my father's young life, it too was not easy. What was their young life like? My father's brother, my uncle Corbin, died from cancer. Father said his brother had terrible headaches, and the doctors could not find medical treatment for him. He passed away in January 1946 at a young age. Father had two sisters who lived to be in their late seventies and eighties.

My father shared his story. His father, my grandfather, worked hard all day. At night, his father made moonshine and sold it. He was told by his father that their mother left them when they were young. The children then had a new mother, a stepmother. She was not a good mother to them. Father said she was mean to the children. And when they would tell their father, he did not believe them.

Father often spoke of his father being strict with the girls and always pushing the boys to hunt and work. His father did not believe in going to school. He needed the children at home to help with housework and the garden.

My father, Garland, said that when he and his only brother were teenagers, he thought he was around sixteen, they got it in their head to end the life of his mean stepmother. The two boys plotted a plan to make this happen. His father, my grandfather, had left for work that day, as he did every day.

They knew the stepmother's schedule and knew she would be outside hanging up clothes, and that was when they would shoot her. They had a fail-proof plan. This was the day they would be free from her. "She would not give us food to eat, and Dad did not believe anything we said about her," he said. The boys often went hunting, so taking their guns and going to the woods was not unusual. They were encouraged to hunt to provide food for the family.

On this particular day, it was warm, and the sun was shining. The two boys went to the perfect place where the stepmother could not see them, and they had a clear view of her. Father said he could not understand why she was not coming out of the house as she did every day. Father said, to this day, he cannot figure out why she did not come out of the house other than the Lord was protecting them from making such a horrible mistake.

Many years went by, then they began to know the real story of what happened to their mother. Their father, our grandfather, never spoke of her. He stuck by the story that she left the family. In later life, my father, Garland, found out that his mother did not leave them, but his father took her away so he could remarry.

Our grandfather placed his wife, my father's mother, and our grandmother, in the Southwestern Virginia Mental Health Institute in Marion, Virginia, on June 12, 1918. The original medical records were destroyed in 1994 in a fire. The medical records director of that institution sent a letter stating she was forty-three years of age and died on May 24, 1921 of acute dysentery. It was said, at that time, Sally was going through a change in life. She did not lose her mind as our grandfather told everyone. What a sad story that someone could do this in the 1900s. The record indicated that for the time she was placed in the asylum, she never had a visitor. The children never knew where she was and never knew where she was buried.

You would think that my father would never have anything to do with his father for the horrible act; however, that would be untrue. His father, our grandfather, came to live with us many years later in Baltimore, Maryland.

Grandpa's physical stature automatically demanded respect and was a bit intimidating. He was a large man, and his weight was well over 250 pounds. He had a mustache and receding hairline. As I was told, he wore bibbed overhauls for casual wear and dress wear.

He was always trying to do things for us when he lived with us. He would say, "I will peel those potatoes," and we would say, "No, Grandpa, you rest." No matter how he tried to help, we stopped him. Looking back, we thought we were helping him, but we were taking his independence away from him.

Needless to say, he didn't stay long in Baltimore, Maryland. He left our home and went to New Jersey to live with other family members. This is where he lived and died around the age of ninety-eight.

I was told that after dinner, the day he died, he went to the porch to watch the sun go down as he rocked in his favorite chair. On this particular day, he watched the last sunset in the western sky.

My maternal grandmother, Sally, was born in 1878 in Virginia. Mother said her parents were so strict. They did not allow the children to dance, sing, or read. If they wanted to learn to read, they could only read the Bible. Grandfather believed the girl's job was to care for the house and care for their husband and their family. Education was the lowest thing on the list to accomplish.

I remember Grandmother sitting in her chair, dressed in a cotton dress, apron over her dress, chewing tobacco, and spitting into her jar. She chewed tobacco until the day she died, she was in her late nineties.

When we visited her, we would get some good food. She always had biscuits in the warmer on the stove. When we walked into the house, we would smell food all the time. Oh my, how good the food was. I can almost smell it now.

She had electricity in her home when I was young and running water in the home; however, we were not allowed to use it. She said, "It cost too much." If you ironed, the iron was sitting on the wood stove or kitchen stove. If you need light, go outside. If you need water, drink from the water that was carried to the house. If you need to use the bathroom, go to the outhouse. When her children had a bathroom put in her house in her older years, she refused to use it. She said it was unsanitary.

We loved to stay at her house when we moved away and came back to visit. She had feather beds. And when you would lie down, you were consumed by the feather mattress and feather blankets. Oh, how wonderful it was. In the morning, around five o'clock, you were awakened by her, "Come and eat." Yes, 5:00 a.m. was get-up time. Oh, the food that she prepared was something I will never forget. Before breakfast, she would also brush her long, silver hair, and it seemed to take her forever. She would take the hair and wrap it around and around until it was up on her head.

We loved our grandmother. She was kind and good; however, we just could not understand why she had such big, long ears. Could she hear better because her ears were so long? To us children, it was a mystery.

We were a little afraid of our paternal grandfather, Tom, I believe, because of his long beard. He was quiet, kind, and gentle, and he loved for us to visit. I recall I was about seven, and we went to visit on a hot summer day. Grandpa came out to greet us, and I was afraid. I quickly locked the doors of the car so he could not get me. My parents were so mad and said to unlock the doors. I refused. I stayed locked in the car until we left their house that day. I remember it being so hot in there. I would roll down the window and get air, then quickly roll it back up. When we got home, guess what I got for this little episode? I don't recall doing this again. I learned my lesson.

When I, Thelma, was about thirteen, we moved from Baltimore back to Virginia. Father was going to work a while in Baltimore while he tried to find employment back in Virginia. Nothing had changed in Virginia from the time we left until now—no work.

We moved into a haunted house. Yes, it was haunted. We heard footsteps, coat hangers swinging in the closet, knocks on the door, and no one was there. Was it the kids' imagination, or was it real? To the children, it was real. We never liked that house. At night, we all slept in the bed with Mother. She would put blankets up at the entrance to the room, and we thought it was to keep the boogeyman out; it was to keep the room warm.

I was depressed because, at this time, I hated Virginia. I pretended to be depressed. I wouldn't come out of the room unless I was forced to do so. I would get up when my mother was gone and run quickly back to bed when she came back.

One day, Mother came running into the house, frightened. She heard us yell "help" three times. When she came running, we said, "We didn't call you. We are fine." Mother was sure one of us was hurt. Later that evening, Mother took off running down the hill to her mother. Yes, Grandpa fell and yelled three times, "Help." We went to the house as the ambulance took him away. He never came out of the hospital.

Before school started that year and after Grandpa passed away, we again moved back to Maryland where our father was still working and living. I was so glad. I had learned to love the city and thought I would never leave the city. Lesson learned, never say never. I remained in the city until 1980 when my husband and I moved to West Virginia.

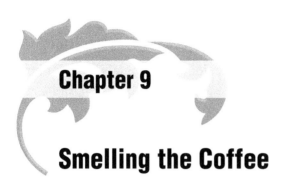

Chapter 9

Smelling the Coffee

The matriarch of the family, my mother, got her very first driver's license at the age of seventy-four years.

Father purchased her a brand-new car, and they bought their first home. They thought that the mobile home was a mansion. They loved it. They had two bathrooms, which they never had before.

Mother would sleep until 11:00 a.m., and Father would get up early, even before sunrise. He would perk coffee. Coffee was not in the drip pots or the Keurig machines. It was the old-fashioned coffee pot. Inside the pot, there is a little metal basket with holes in it where you place the coffee, you place the lid on the basket, place the basket on the long stem, and place it inside the pot. Of course, you fill the pot with water and place the stem into the pot. Then you would hear the bubbling as the water heats, and the coffee perks. As I write the book, I can hear the pot perking, and I can smell the aroma of that fresh pot of coffee, just made to perfection.

I can also hear the sound of the bacon frying in the pan. When the bacon was fried, and the coffee had perked, you were then awakened to the voice of a tall, thin man with a balding head, saying, "Get up, you sleepyhead. You are going to sleep your life away," then he would proceed to tell you he had bacon and coffee ready. He would leave the room and know that you were going to get up. In about ten minutes, if your feet were not on the floor, you would get that same visitor again. "Get up, you sleepyhead. You are going to sleep your life away." After about four times of this visitor, you would roll out of that bed.

He then would tell you what a beautiful morning it was and how glad to be alive. At that time, you could just care less. You did not want the coffee or bacon; you just wanted to sleep until noon. But that was just out of the question.

Being from a poor family and no education and only minimum-pay jobs his whole life, I always worried about how they would get by financially as they aged. How could they survive when they got older? I was married, and I would often cry myself to sleep, worrying about their future. Mother would say, "I don't worry about it. Jesus will take care of us. I don't know how, but he will. Don't worry." Keep reading and you will see how they survived as they aged.

My father and I worked at the same company for many years. My first job was when I was in the ninth grade of school, and I worked there for many years.

Father struggled to breathe and lots of days could not go to work. I decided I had to get him help. My parents had no health insurance and no money. At this time, they lived in a small rented apartment in Baltimore, Maryland.

I went to organizations in hopes of getting them some financial help, and they were always rejected. One agency said, "They have children. They can care for them." It was true; however, none of the children were in a good financial position to help them. The children helped as best as they could. They helped to buy food and pay their bills as I tried to get him medical attention.

My father had been out of the coal mines for many years, but there was word he may be eligible for black lung benefits. We researched and, with the doctor's help, applied, and after a couple of years, he was approved for benefits and received a check. These funds continued until his death.

Mother said, "See, I told you God would take care of us." What a powerful message. She had no other resources; she must depend on God. He provided for them so many times in their life, Mother would say. They had anything and everything they wanted or needed until their deaths.

What a mighty God we serve!

Chapter 10

Heartbreak and Trouble

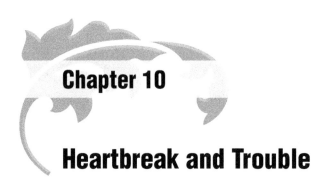

Child number 3, Shirley, had a great desire to help incarcerated individuals. She understood their challenges since her first son was often incarcerated. My nephew started down the wrong path around the age of thirteen. He first began the fall by not attending school. Then he got into gambling. He felt that he was going to hit it big one day. He would go to the horse racetrack instead of going to school. After gambling got hold of his life, drugs, and drug dealers were showing up at his house and business. He was the owner of a popular pawnshop in Greenville, South Carolina, for several years.

For years, he was in and out of jail. I recall being told on many occasions, he was beaten so badly and even hospitalized by bad police officers. During his lifetime, he left several broken wives and children. At the time of his death, he had four children and four living siblings. In his final years, his mother said, "He's a good boy now, but his body is wrecked from a life of bad living." Drinking, drugs, you name it, and he did it. He was talkative and handsome and loved by his first wife deeply. They had two children. She stuck by him as long as she could, until one day she had to leave to protect the children.

He was living in Tennessee and was to come to South Carolina in December for two court hearings. His mother had written him and conveyed the court date had been delayed from December until late January. He did not get this letter since he had moved. He went to South Carolina in December, thinking he had an upcoming court appearance. He got a hotel room, and he thought he would be going to court the next day. Needless to say, he did not go to court. He was found the next day on the bed in the hotel, deceased. The medical examiner's report said it was alcohol poisoning. He was fifty-eight years of age. Later, it was discovered that he had called his mother, and the phone had been disconnected since she got a new phone. He left his very last message on that phone, and there, in the hotel room, the state police found him.

As this family has had many tragedies, the biggest tragedy is that they lost their way. When my nephew died, his mother could not attend the funeral; she was too ill, and his sister and brothers could not attend.

There were ex-wives, children, friends, and other family members there; however, the folks he grew up with, and whom he felt were his strongest supporters, were not there. Ask yourself, is this the road that I want to take?

When my nephew was just a child and going down the wrong pathway, he thought he was having fun. Later in life, he said he never thought his life would have been like it was. He was racked with pains, full of drugs, and sickness, full of hurts, dishonoring himself and his family, being distrusted by family, and he was full of heartbreak. He disgraced his family, grandparents, and children. Even though in his last years he was sorry for what he had done to himself and everyone, especially his children whom he loved deeply, he just didn't show it to them. He didn't know how to love. He was so broken physically and mentally, and he realized it was too late to mend fences with anyone other than his mother.

My sister loved the nightlife. She would take advantage of any man that she met since it was money that she was after. "I had to have money to take care of my children since I made so little and had no one to help me." She remembers one man who had purchased a ruby ring for his wife, and she took him up on the offer to spend time with him. She remembers how she had rules before getting involved passionately. He was to shower first. She said, while he was in the shower, she took all his money from his wallet and the ruby ring. She left while he was showering and never saw him again. She took the money and purchased a television for her son and daughter to have something to watch.

Another story was she fell deeply in love with a very handsome kind man, who said he had not been married before. They spent time together and got married, but in a short while, she became pregnant, and the man did not want any children. When she told him of the pregnancy, she left for work that morning. And when she returned home that night, his clothes and belongings were gone. She never saw him again. Yes, she had a beautiful female child, and what a blessing was given to us.

After two children and working long hours, she married men that she did not love. She married so she would have money to support her children. Out of the nine men she married, only two were good to her, and she loved them. They never beat her. All the other men would beat her and knock her down with their fists. She had many bruises and broken bones. She didn't tell anyone; she was ashamed. She tried to hide it from her children and family.

She would work to the point of collapse. She would be so tired most of the time. She would laugh and carry on like everything was great; however, inside she was broken, weak, frail, and so fragile. She said, if it were not for her children, she would have died many times; they kept her going. She just kept giving and working. She tried to give the children everything that she could; however, she indicated that she failed them miserably.

The one husband that she loved so much, and they seemed to be so happy, abandoned her too. She was pregnant when he said he was leaving with a fifteen-year-old that he had met. She begged him not to leave them. What was she going to do? How could she raise these children alone? She was out of her mind, desperate, and lost. The only thing she could think to do was to abort this child she was carrying. She said she took a pencil and stuck it up inside her. She did not believe in abortion; however, when you are in a desperate position, you often do things that you regret later. At the time, the only puzzle pieces she had gave her this only recourse of action.

Her husband came, put the family in the car, and drove the family to his sister in Alabama, and then he left them. Shirley began getting sick. She ended up in the hospital, had a miscarriage, and was in a coma for twelve days. The doctor kept asking, "What did you do?" She said, "I kept saying nothing."

She pulled through this sickness. And when she began to get well enough to travel, his sister called her brother to come and get his family. A few days later, the brother and husband picked them up, and he then took them back to Baltimore to his other sister's home. This sister cared for several foster children, and she had no room for them to stay for any length of time.

Again, she was alone with five children: two from a previous marriage and three boys by him. As she got better and settled in. She would not leave her ex-husband and his new wife alone. One day she thought, *I will take the kids to him and see if he and his new wife can care for them.* This was to punish him for a while.

Children are hard to raise with two parents, let alone one. What a mistake that was! She left the children with him that day, and they packed up and moved. She began tracking them down, time after time, to get her children. And time and time again, they moved. She had no money and no way to fight for them, except to follow them around, year in and year out.

Over time, the children forgot her, and she never saw them for a very long time. If she did see them, it would only be for a few minutes. From this time on, she was extremely angry with men and hurt continually. This also changed her life forever.

There are so many details, trips, and encounters that only she could tell. You can relate if you have ever been in this type of situation, she would say.

Fathers and mothers who have been divorced can relate to this. If they do not have custody, they cannot see their children as they would like to. This is caused by so much anger and hurt between the spouses. Often the spouse that does not have custody has very limited visitation. The children don't understand when the other parent is not there day and night. She said, "It wasn't that I did not want to see them." She often could not find them. She also felt that she committed murder, and God would never forgive her. She only drifted further away from family and God.

For the next eighteen years, Shirley was not in contact with any of the family. The family would call her children, and they would tell us how Shirley was doing. Finally, one day, the eighth-born child, Thelma, decided, "No more. If I do not hear from Shirley directly, and I gave a specific date for her to respond to me, you will then be reported to the FBI as a missing person." I was sure her lifestyle did not want police in her life. Within a very short time, she sent up-to-date photographs of herself, and they reeked with cigarette smoke, and we knew it was her. She included ten photographs of the same picture with a note to each child. Within a short period, she contacted child number 8, Thelma, and she began to communicate with all of the family until her death. Lee did not welcome her back into the family. He felt she walked away from us, and she just wanted us to forget, he said.

Several years before her death, she married a man who had never been married, had no children, and was retired from the navy. She lived a very good, happy, and successful life with him for another twenty years. She placed all of her attention, time, and money into community work, nonprofits, education, and public speaking at civic venues, obtaining a nonprofit charter, and businesses, just to name a few things. Her prison work was a calling, she said.

During all of these hard times, she married nine times. Two of the husbands, she married twice. She had six children: one girl and five boys. She said, "I wanted to be like two people I had heard about, Elizabeth Taylor and I was able to do that by marriage and wanted to be like Scarlett O'Hara and say, 'I will never be hungry again.'" She never was.

She said she loved only two of the husbands; the others were a way to survive. The two she loved never beat or mistreated her; all the other men abused her terribly. Many times, she was in and out of the hospital with broken bones and bruises. Many times, she stayed inside the house for weeks being so broken and bruised, which also meant she could not go to work and therefore had no money or would lose her job.

What helped her was that everyone who met her loved her. Every employer loved her and her work ethic. She could always find work; it just didn't pay enough to provide for her family.

Even in her most distressed time, if you called her and asked for any kind of help, she responded and would give away anything she had to that person in need. She sent money, gifts, cards, airplane tickets, hotel reservations, clothing, and food to anyone who asked. She would say, "The Lord will help me get more for my family. They probably need it more than me."

Chapter 11

Death Knocked Again

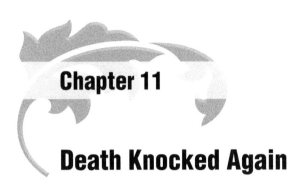

My sister Shirley had one female child. This daughter had many successes and many heartaches. She was married to the man of her dreams and looking forward to a great life together.

They purchased a beautiful large home in an upscale neighborhood. The day came, and they closed on the house and held the keys to their new home. It is my understanding, that very day, her husband chartered an airplane and flew on a business trip. On the return trip, the weather turned bad. Not seeing the mountain in front of them, the pilot flew into a mountain. Her husband was killed immediately.

Time passed, and she struggled to move forward. As time passed, the day came when she met another man with whom she thought they would be happy together. They traveled, went on cruises, and was enjoying life. Life again was at its best; however, that too would be short-lived.

As I understand it, he was coming home and went around a curve, struck a bridge, and was killed instantly. Again, a young woman had two tragic events in a few short years.

Again, she struggled to get better and raise her one and only son. During the deepest time in life, she began to drink, drink, and drink. She struggled for many years, looking for happiness and peace. It seemed that it alluded her. She tried to focus on raising her son, and she succeeded. Soon he was in college and studying to become a doctor. Her son graduated, married, and moved to Virginia. In 2019, I heard that her son had passed away from an illness. What a tragedy! I ask how one person can survive when all odds seem to be against her. The answer is that you do what she had done: pull yourself up and move forward.

You can survive. She is loved, thought of, and prayed for continually by all those who love her. She is a beautiful person inside and outside. I would also add kind, good, and funny.

Her mother, Shirley, said, "I tried to help her, but when you are broken yourself and full of pain, you are no help. We both were in desperate need of healing. She was so young and so broken by life."

She said, "I know you still wonder why I ran away from the family. As you listen to the tapes I have left for you, you will see how broken I was and could not find peace, even when death knocked on my door many times."

Her prescription medication started her down the pathway to drugs, and she said, "I was so ashamed. I was hooked and could not do without the drugs. I did not want the family to know, so I left them and never communicated with any of them for eighteen years."

She said all she thought about was the green: money. She knew how to get it. She thought, *If I get out of this way of life, I'll not have any money anymore and can't buy the things I want.* She enjoyed what she did, and she didn't want to get out of it. She loved the nightlife and loved to party. She said she never cared for alcohol, so she drank very little. "The nightlife was fun for years," she said. "However, looking back now, it was not worth it. It was not real happiness."

You see, she was bound by the devil, and he had total control of her. She knew she needed to be delivered by Jesus, whom she had been taught about in her younger life. She said, "Jesus would not help me. I am too bad." She believed that, so she didn't ask for his help for a long time.

Tragedy struck again. Death came to Shirley's pride and joy, her three-year-old son. He had a staph infection, and his little body could not overcome the infection. What a sad day. In those days, many people had their loved ones laid out in their homes. This was done for this child. He laid on top of their large radio/record player cabinet. This practice seems strange today; however, in the 1950s and 1960s this was a common practice.

When there was a death in the family, usually a wreath was placed on the door of their home so people would know they were in mourning. There was one on this home as well. As time passed, my sister accepted Christ as her Savior and was freed from drugs and alcohol. She became a new person. She turned her life around. She attended college and became a businesswoman and a pillar in the community in South Carolina. She became a spokesperson and advocate for those who could not speak for themselves. She received many awards and recognition from the state she lived in. She had a charter in South Carolina and helped families affected by incarcerated persons.

She had a passion for the prisoners and their families when they were released from prison. She helped them get back into society. She helped many who were out of jail to find a home, job, money, and clothes for themselves and their children. "It was a calling," she said. She has had many stories of successful persons released back into society, and she took pride in the work she accomplished with them.

There were many she thought were innocent and later found out she was wrong. Many were guilty and had done horrendous things. She recalled many horrible stories of killing, rape, children killing their parents, and killing of prostitutes. One person she helped to get him established outside of jail, got a job, got a place to live, and ultimately, he raped her. She was so broken from this horrible experience. It too affected her life. She said, "Only someone that has been raped can relate to it. Rape is different than me sleeping with men. I have encountered the devil himself through different people and experiences. I have walked through this life, and the devil walked me. The Lord took his hand off of me, and I went through the drugs and wild life and the men in my life and abandoned by the love of my life, my children."

In life, for a very long time, she blamed all her troubles on someone other than herself. She realized she was wrong—they were not the reason for her behavior. She wanted to repay her mother and father for her life of poverty. For some reason, she thought it was their choice to be poor and blamed them. "I was not a good daughter to them. I'm sorry for that," she said. She worked so hard to provide for her children; she had no support. She hurt them so badly with her behavior. She said, "I am so sorry for the pain that I caused all of them. I wish I could see them now before I die and tell them how sorry I am and how proud I am of what they have become."

After years of bad behavior and telling lies about anything and everything, you could not believe a word she said. She would swear it was the truth and know that she was not telling the truth. She did not want people to know the real person she was. "I am like an alcoholic. I had to admit my failures and ask God to help me out of the mess that I alone created.

After many years of this type of behavior, doctors discovered she had a chemical imbalance in the brain. And when she began taking the medicine, she became a different person.

All her life, she was a giver, and people that met her loved her. She was such a hard worker. She was fun to be with. She was funny. She was beautiful. She was a caring and giving person to anyone that she saw. She was a go-getter. If she focused on something to achieve, she accomplished it.

God will help people in their time of need if they ask, and we, the people, need to help those who are struggling. We must help them see that there are good reasons to change. Most people think they would like to change; however, many don't want to change. Their actions betray them. Their action and words conflict.

When you want to change, you will! Instead of putting those who have habits and struggles down or talking about how bad we think they are, let us pray and support them. You or I may be the person that will change their life forever. Pointing fingers and making allegations do not help.

People don't just tell their problems; they don't want it to be out on the street. If we listen, God's spirit will let us know how to help that person in need. We must listen to that small, still voice. Satan is good at his job. His job is to rob you, kill you, and destroy you and everyone that is in his path.

My sister hid from the truth. She thought *I had to be bad before I could be good.* What a silly statement for her to hold on to.

She realized a house is only a house until you make it a home. If you don't take care of the house, it will decay and fall. A house that becomes a home will have the breeze flow through it, heat in the winter, and cool in the summer—a place of peace, joy, and relaxation. She found this place in her later life.

So sad, she wasted so many years of her life. Little did she know how spiritually blind she was. With all the prison work she was doing, with all of the counseling she was doing, she was doing what she was trying to help others overcome. She said, "I couldn't help it. I was addicted. I had to have it. No one knew it but me and the drug dealers."

My sister raised the children, or did the children raise themselves? This could be open for discussion with the family. I am sure it was both ways.

Remember, your decision will not only affect you, it will affect generation after generation.

Sometimes children want to blame their decision on their parents for being raised in dysfunctional families. Stop! Sure you can blame anyone you want. You also can grab yourself by the shirt collar and say, "I am going to be different," and you will be different. If you place goodness in front of you, set your eyes on the prize of peace and prosperity, health and happiness, and stay focused. With God's help, you will overcome any obstacles that come your way.

When my sister decided to come back into the family after eighteen years of being estranged, she said, "My brothers and their wives came to visit me, and it made me feel so, so good. They showed me that they always loved me. It was me that dropped from their life for eighteen years. My brothers always tried to protect me in my young life; I just didn't see it then. I was on the fast track, but now I'm on the slow track. I have had a wild life, and I wish I could call back and change things."

Shirley said, "I'm that poor girl who got to be a rich little girl, who was miserable until I forgave myself of my past and asked Christ to forgive me for letting him down, and Jesus is the answer to all problems. Oh, Lord, if I would have only opened my heart and eyes sooner. He said he would never leave or forsake me, and now I know he never left me. *I left him.*"

She was known for years as Ole Lady Haney, who owned several businesses in the Carolinas and helped people through their difficult times with her nonprofit organization, the other side of the road.

I ponder, *What else will these tapes she left me reveal?* I have only begun to understand her pain—being in and out of institutions; being shot at several times; children struggling with habits, trying to drown their pain from the life they have endured; miscarriages; death; her taking advantage of every wealthy man she encountered; falling in love; abandonment; riches; diamonds; cars; travel; businesses; counseling; nonprofit work. On the tape, she said, "It feels like I have lived two lifetimes, I don't know that person. Was I two persons?"

As the lines of her life ran through the mountains, she had a mother and a grandmother. I wonder if she asked them for guidance. Did she think I was right? They are old and don't know what they are talking about. Often, when we are young, we do not realize those persons who have lived longer than us, teenagers, usually have more wisdom and knowledge than they do.

In your time of struggle, ask your grandma or someone you trust and respect for guidance. If you use and follow it, it will keep you on the right road all the days of your life. Sometimes people hire lawyers to tell them what to do in certain situations. And when the lawyer tells them what they think they should do, often the person who hired them does not take their advice seriously. Would you be one of these people receiving advice?

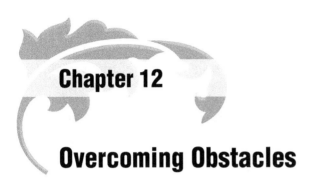

Chapter 12

Overcoming Obstacles

Don't blame others for your life; you are responsible for it. That's what this young lady you are about to read about would tell you.

A caseworker for the state of West Virginia, a friend, asked if I would go to a location with her to interview two children who were in temporary foster care. They were staying with a distant aunt and uncle, who indicated that due to illness, they could no longer care for the children. The caseworker would be placing them in a more permanent location. The caseworker was doing the talking, and I was watching the children playing, while my heart was aching for them. After a few hours, the caseworker said she would be in touch. We left the home with heavy hearts. The parents were out of the picture. The father had previously passed away. The mother was on drugs and alcohol and was out of the picture.

The caseworker explained the situation of one healthy child and one child with cerebral palsy and the challenge she was facing in placing both of the children in the same home. Most foster families did not want a physically challenged child. She could place the healthy child, not the physically challenged child. She was holding off on placement for one child since she did not want to split the two sisters up.

On our drive back home, the caseworker said, "You have a large home. Would you consider helping me out for a little while? No more than three months."

I said, "Oh, no, I don't think so. I don't think I could do that. I have to work, and my husband has a business. Our children are grown". I thought, *Why I would want to do that?*

Before we departed each other's company, I agreed to ask my husband if he would consider caring for the children for no more than three months, just until the caseworker could find a suitable home for the children.

After being dropped off at my husband's business, my husband, Tom, and I headed home. During our twenty-minute ride, I said, "Do you want to start another family?"

He first chuckled and said, "Are you pregnant?" Of course, the answer was *no*, then I began to explain. His first response was, "No, why would I want to do that? Our children are grown, and now we have grandchildren."

I nervously laughed, then I shared my story of the two children that I met that day. He was not thrilled about taking in two children; nonetheless, one was severely challenged.

My husband is a special man. He has a heart of gold. He is a kind, compassionate, and caring individual. And as I explained the children's situation, he answered, "Whatever you want to do is okay with me. I hate to see the girls split up. What if that was our children?"

The children's mother was still alive; however, she had no visitation rights, and she was still on drugs and alcohol and could not care for herself.

My husband and I were about to undertake this challenge. As the days passed, we attended and completed all of the training and state requirements to get certified to take in foster children. We purchased two single beds and prepared our bedroom for our new children. The day arrived. The van came down the driveway with two little girls and a few trash bags that carried all they owned; it was sad. We chatted with the distant uncle and aunt, and it was now time for the uncle and aunt to leave these two children with two total strangers. Little did the children know, this was only a temporary placement.

The children settled into their rooms for that night. Over the next few days, our grown children and our grandchildren came with their families and met the two young girls, who were now sleeping in their old bedrooms. Our children and grandchildren immediately accepted them, and the two girls became part of our family. They were treated no differently than our children, and each of our children treated them as sisters. As the days went by, the girls were enrolled in their new school, and they started a new life. They adapted quickly to their new surroundings. The healthy preteen was a wonderful housekeeper, cook, and care provider for the physically challenged child.

Melissa did not ask for anything; all she did was give. She worked continually. Never did she leave anything sitting around. Never did she not make the bed, wash her clothes, and do anything else she saw that needed attention. She was mature in so many ways, and her speech was like an adult. She had some limitations in school, and we believed it was partially due to her upbringing. We all have obstacles to overcome, and that we did, over came with victory.

One night, everyone was in bed, and I heard the healthy preteen child crying. I went into the bedroom and asked, "Sweetie, what is wrong?" She called me by name and said, "You won't keep us. No one will because of my sister." We talked for a while, and I shared with her we would cross that bridge later on. She calmed down, and I gave her a tight hug and kiss on the forehead, said a prayer, and I went back to bed.

When I got back to my bedroom, I think I cried all night. Then one day led to another, one month to another month, one year to another year until Melissa, at the age of 18, left home to marry and have a life of her own.

The six-year-old had severe cerebral palsy. She could not walk, could not do anything for herself. She was spastic and did not have the freedom to move her arms and hands much. She could not do the American sign language. She created her own signs to communicate with grunting and making sounds. The child protective service thought she was about two or three years old in the mind.

Just picture this small-framed girl, well under the size and weight for her age. Her legs were tight and bent at the knee. She could not stand or straighten her legs out. Her little hands were curved. Her lips were curved. And her brown hair was coarse and wavy. The haircut was short around the ears, and the cut squared off in the back at the collar line. She had a very stubborn hair cowlick that just would not allow her hair to style easily.

She loved to have makeup, perfume, and body lotion on her body. I would put lotion on her tiny arms so she could smell it. She would be so happy and say I love you with her quiet language.

She would crawl on her knees, and, boy, could she do that. She would get out of the chair, get on those hands and knees, and off she would go down the four-foot wide hallway and climb into her bed. She loved to sleep. If you would let her, she would stay there all day and night.

She would only get up to tell you, "I'm hungry." She did this by rubbing her stomach, taking her hand and placing it up to her mouth. When we would feed her, she needed to be fed very slowly, otherwise she would choke. It would take a good hour to feed her at one feeding. One of her greatest pleasures was to eat and eat again!

Once you got to know her own sign language, you could communicate and understand what she wanted. One thing she did not lack was hearing. You could talk about her or situations, and she would let you know she knew what you were talking about. She also knew when you were going to go in the car for a ride or go shopping. She would crawl and get her coat or just crawl out the door and be ready to go. When you would take her shopping, she wanted to go to the shoe department. You could pick up a pair of shoes. And if she did not like them, she would squeal and throw them on the floor. So you see, she could understand; however, there was no way to tell how much she understood or what her level of understanding was since she could not verbally communicate.

Let's get back to the healthy young child. She was so beautiful, and her smile was intoxicating. During this time, their father, who loved them very much, could not take care of them due to his limitations. This healthy little girl cooked, cleaned, cared for her father, nursed him, clothed her sister, and carried her to the bus stop on her back. They would get on the bus and go off to school. Time went by, and the healthy child continued to care for her severely physically challenged sister and her father, who had his legs amputated due to diabetes, until his death.

As I understand it, this little girl was taking food from school and carrying it home since they had little to live on. One day, a teacher noticed this, and it is my understanding that a caring teacher led the state agency to help these children. The state removed them from the mother and placed them in a distant aunt's home, who was ill and could not keep them for any extended time. This is how they ultimately came to live in our home.

The time came when the young lady left our home to start a life of her own. We continued to care for her sister. Time came when the state could not provide respite for us since both of us were always employed. You see, a lot of foster families have one of the parents work from home.

This was not our case—we both were employed outside of the home. When the children arrived, my husband had his own business, so he was able to put the children on the school bus, and the bus dropped them off at his store. It worked well.

There came a time when my husband closed his business and took another position that required him to be like others and go to work for someone else. Therefore, we had no one to get the child off the bus or place her on the bus. The state could not provide services to help us. We traveled down a very difficult path trying to resolve these issues for quite a while.

Finally, the day came when we could no longer work with these situations, and our precious baby was taken to another placement. While she was in placement with another family, we still went and took her on vacations, respite often, and saw her continually. This all occurred until 2015, when I became sick myself and could no longer care for her.

The healthy, child is in her forties with a family of her own. We have foster grandchildren who are very much a part of our family and always will be our daughters and grandchildren. She has three healthy children: one boy and two girls.

Our healthy foster daughter has worked hard, raising her children as a single parent. She acquired her certified nursing assistant (CNA) status and works in nursing homes, caring for people who can't care for themselves; I bet she is excellent at her job.

There are obstacles in life; however, if our child could overcome this and be successful, don't tell me you can't. Could it be your attitude? Don't blame others. Don't blame your upbringing. Don't blame the alcoholic parents for the hurt you have experienced; it is not easy to overcome pain and hurt for sure, but it can be accomplished.

You may never be able to respect or obey your parents, family, or those who took care of you. Maybe they never did anything to deserve your respect. *You* must find a way to move on, even though you feel you can't or don't want to. Let this day be the day of a new beginning! Fake it until you make it if you must. You can do it!

Don't follow in their footsteps. Let's make it together. And with your "can do" attitude and God's help, you will succeed! You will always have an attitude. You will either choose to have a good attitude or a bad attitude; it will be your choice which you choose to embrace and adopt as your motto for the rest of your life.

Hard times can either make you better, or it can make you bitter. Remember, it is never too late or too soon to change.

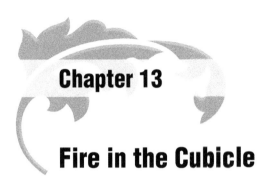

Chapter 13

Fire in the Cubicle

Overcoming obstacles is obtainable. You must be willing to work at it every day. If you are not tired of what you are doing, the life you live, and the habits you have, you will not change or give them up. If you truly want freedom, there is help in today's world if you cannot do it on your own.

I have seen people who were extremely bound by drugs, alcohol, abusive behavior, tempers, and downright mean, and they conquered their pain, habits, and addiction on their own with the conviction to overcome and that they can with God's help. I have seen alcoholics walk away totally on their own and become a different person.

I watched my father, who smoked Camel cigarettes all his life. The doctor told him, "You quit smoking, and I will help you. If you don't quit, don't come back to me." Father and I left the doctor's office that day, and there was a street trash can on the sidewalk. There he stopped, reached into his shirt pocket, took out his pack of Camel cigarettes, tossed them into the trash can, and said "I will never smoke another one as long as I live," and he never smoked again.

With God, and sometimes doctors, you can overcome those obstacles that keep you tied down. Miracles can take place in your life. It's not easy but it is obtainable, and you can be victorious. You are not the first with addictions, and you will not be the last. However, failure is not an option!

Another person, who you are about to read about, overcame impossible odds, so can you! My brother, child number 10, Roger Ray (April 1, 1952), has traveled around the world and across the United States for forty years, working mostly in coal and nuclear power plants.

Roger began working for the General Electric company when he was nineteen years of age. At the age of twenty-four, while working at the Baltimore, Maryland, General Electric plant, he had the opportunity with the company to work on a government contract the company had acquired at the Washington Naval Yard at government contract pay. He was married and had two children, and taking this job paid more than working locally. He jumped at the opportunity to make more money to support his family.

He stated, "In those days, there was almost no training, even for a job with such great responsibility. The training consisted mainly of learning from others and learning as you worked on the job. There was some formal training."

Thursday, November 13, 1975, was no different than any other day. Roger, his wife, and children awakened around 5:00 a.m., and each prepared for their day's busy schedule. Roger would drive his pickup truck and stop at the local coffee shop for his favorite morning coffee. After picking up his favorite drink, he then would drive onto the Baltimore and Washington, DC beltway, and there would find himself in heavy traffic, all the way to his job site at the Washington Naval Yard.

Upon arriving at his job site, he would change clothes, get his tools out of his heavy tool bag, mask in hand, hard hat on his head, and off to the assigned workstation. He recalls it was around 9:30 a.m. when he was to work in a high-voltage cubicle that had been tested, and he was told the power was off, but it wasn't. There were 13,800 volts of electricity running through those lines. He believes an arc of electricity went through his fingers, hands, and across the heart and exited his finger that was on the floor. He was on fire and was thrown twenty feet or so in the air. A coworker saw Roger on fire and tossed into the air. His coworker quickly jumped into action and was able to put the fire out that was consuming Roger's body. This most likely restarted Roger's heart. His coworker was badly burned, and he was taken to the hospital also. Needless to say, my brother was in shock. He remembers getting up from the floor, going to the bathroom, and seeing himself in a mirror burned black. He couldn't believe his eyes. He was burned so badly, and he feared he would be disfigured for life. The ambulance arrived, and he walked to the ambulance. He said, "I was not in pain." In reality, he was in shock and unaware of the pain he was experiencing. He remembers waking up in the hallway of the Washington, DC, hospital, and he wanted to go home to Baltimore, where his family was.

Child number 9, my brother, Larry Garland (June 12, 1949), recalls he received a call he believed came from the hospital in Washington, DC, saying that his brother had been severely burned and would not be expected to live. I too received the same call. I left my job and headed to the DC hospital too. It was a race against time.

When Larry and I arrived at the hospital, our brother was lying in the hallway, and he was unrecognizable. We first walked by him; we did not recognize him. His hands were larger than boxing gloves, his body burned black, and no one was working on him. *Why?* we thought.

Larry called a doctor he trusted for guidance and asked what he would recommend for him to do to get Roger to a burn center in hopes of saving his life. Larry shared the story with that doctor, who called other doctors and the hospital to prepare them to receive our brother. Roger's wife consented to the transfer from Washington Hospital to St. Agnes Hospital in Baltimore, Maryland. This transfer was against the doctor's wishes at the Washington Hospital. Upon arrival at St. Agnes Hospital in Maryland, the doctors performed emergency surgery on his arms to allow the swelling to go down. The surgeons cut his arms from the armpit to the tip of his index fingers, and the cuts were left open for days, allowing the swelling to recede, in hopes of saving his arms, which they saved.

At this time, he spent three months in the hospital, isolated from everyone. You could speak to him through a speaker on the door and see him through the glass room that he was placed in.

The pain he endured was more than any human could take, and somehow he took it. He recalls the pain when the doctors and nurses would wrap him in bandages, leave them on for a few days, put him in a tub of ice water, and then rip the bandages off, pulling off the dead skin with the bandages. The nurses were not finished, and they would scrape the burn to remove other dead skin. This was done over and over again each time the bandages were changed. This process was performed to clean away the dead skin and prepare the area for skin grafts. The doctors would remove the skin from other parts of the body and place that skin in the burnt area: his eyelids, ears, face, hands, arms, and anywhere the body was burned. Once skin graft surgery was completed, other parts of the body were raw and sore.

He recalls receiving pain injections continually since he could not endure the pain. He and the family were afraid he would become addicted to the drugs, and they were correct. He became addicted. Now he had another challenge to overcome: the addiction. Yet during this painful time, his thoughts were of his family. He remembers thinking his hospitalization and being out of work, was going to be rough on the family, especially since this accident occurred so close to the holidays, Thanksgiving and Christmas just weeks away. Roger was going through physical pain and also mental pain for his family. The journey of pain, hardships, and recovery was just the beginning. "How do I pay the mortgage? How do I buy food? How do I buy Christmas gifts for the children?"

This was the beginning of a very long and hard road ahead for him and his family. For the next several years, he was in and out of the hospital for surgeries. He can't recall how many skin grafts and surgeries he had. He believes it exceeded ten major surgeries

Against the doctor's orders, Roger went back to work two years after the accident; however, he was terrified of power and found it difficult to work at General Electric. He left that employer and went to work at a smaller company for about four years, not working with electricity.

As time passed, he decided to go back to work at General Electric to overcome his fears of working with electricity and continue to face his health issues. He knew he could travel, and his income would be higher with more finances to support his family. It was difficult to enter back into the same field of work that almost cost him his life;

however, he was determined to overcome his fears and do the job he loved. He said, "Even today, fear grips me when I am near high-voltage electric." He worked and retired from the company after thirty-seven years.

"Throughout the years, money was no object. It was easy to make money if you wanted to work hard. There were lots of times when I worked away from home and long hours. And in doing so, I sacrificed time with my family," he said.

During the early years, after the burn, the family's struggles were many. Ultimately, it cost him his first marriage, and divorce itself brought about a lot of unwelcome baggage that he had to face. Being away from his two children was the greatest challenge.

As the years passed, he met his second wife in Baltimore, Maryland. As a youngster, she lived on the same street in Baltimore as we did. Roger and his second wife were playmates as children.

In 1994, the Baltimore General Electric office closed. Roger then transferred to Cincinnati, Ohio, office for the next nine years. Roger became tired of staying in hotels, and he purchased an RV (recreational vehicle) to live in, and then he and his wife began looking for a place to build a retirement home.

During these years, his wife traveled back and forth to Florida, where she purchased land and contracted to have their home built. Roger continued to work in Cincinnati and commute to Florida as often as possible for nine years.

After nine years, another opportunity in Jacksonville, Florida, opened, and he was able to transfer closer to home. Here he worked for the next five years and was able to go home to Florida on the weekends since he was only three hours away from home. The Jacksonville office closed after five years, and the company offered him an early retirement package, and he took it.

He has not fully retired. He loves to work, and works hard he does. He says, "I don't have any problems with my burns, just feel self-conscious sometimes." He has few regrets in life. He has beautiful homes and all of the trimmings, a great family, children, and grandchildren. With the doctors, family support, and God, he is alive and well. One of his greatest joys is telling jokes. When you are with him, you will laugh the majority of the time. He has a great outlook on life and takes good care of his body. He believes that laughter is good medicine, and he fills his and other people's days with just that: laughter!

Chapter 14

A Service of Love

As I reflect on my own life, I am amazed and often wonder how I was able to have such a good life and wonderful opportunities given to a woman who came from such humble beginnings to a person whom some would call an ambassador.

I often say, my life resembles the life of Joseph in the Bible. He was sold into slavery by his own family and rose to a place of authority. My family did not sell me; however, due to a lack of education and finance, I was not pointed to a higher education or to pursue any career. Just work and get a paycheck, and you will be successful! I was directed to work hard, and I worked hard, beginning at the age of fifteen until I retired in 2017. Let us begin with my story.

I, Thelma Jene (December 15, 1946), took the road to the right, and my sister, Shirley, took the road to the left, as you have previously read. You will see that we took two very different pathways.

I have been married to my husband since 1965, and I love him dearly, and often you may hear me say, "After all these years, I still like him." Yes, that is so true. So many people, when they are together for so long, fall out of love; they survive. This is not my case. I still live a fairy-tale dream. Please don't wake me!

My husband is an honorable, hardworking man. I met him when I was twelve years old in Baltimore, Maryland. When he graduated high school in West Virginia, he came to Maryland to live with his parents and attend the University of Maryland School of Drafting.

He began a career at a book bindery, paying his way through college. He purchased a black 1957 Chevrolet car with red and black interior. He polished, shinned, and worked on the car all of the time. He loved that car as most young men do. He then began a career with General Motors Corporation, retired, and started a sporting goods and taxidermy business for the next thirty-five years.

He then worked as a government contractor. He was a hard worker, day in and day out working from early morning and often until midnight, caring for his family.

He provides a great living for his family. In addition to physically working for his family, he was, and is, truly a dedicated man to a higher power in his life. He said, "As for me and my household, we will serve the Lord." That he does and did his entire life.

He set high standards for our family, and we lived up to those standards with his guidance and the Lord at our side. When I saw my sister's pathway, I did not want to travel that road. I prayed as a young girl for the Lord to give me a person in my life who would serve him and not have habits or baggage that would hinder our perfect life together. My husband had not been previously married, nor did he have any children, and he had accepted Jesus as his Lord and Savior and made a commitment that he would serve him all the days of his life on that Valentine's Day in Baltimore, Maryland. How could I go wrong?

As time passed, and we began thinking of being a couple, my father, who had not attended any of the children's weddings, said, "He is a good man and will take good care of you. I will go to your wedding." *What?* That was amazing. My father saw the man that he approved of for his youngest daughter, and child number 8 was about to leave his home and become the adult that he and his wife had raised.

Let's begin with today and go back to childhood as I remember it. After retirement, my husband, Tom, and I had the privilege to travel and see the beautiful world God has created and see many beautiful places, including visiting our homeland of Scotland and Ireland.

We traveled extensively until COVID hit the United States. Travel came to a halt. These travels bring back many memories of places; however, the most memorable times are those where human-to-human contact occur daily, and relationships grow into friendships. Let me share a few wonderful memories of my life.

Today, after twenty-five years of service, I am retired from the Department of the Interior (DOI.) I work approximately eighty-five miles outside of our beautiful capitol, Washington, DC, at what I will call a center. The center "created a climate where people of all disciplines—government, academic, corporate, nonprofit—come together to learn skills, break down barriers, and share perspectives." The center is a world-class training center where people from all over the world come to share, learn, and do strategic planning for agencies, state, local, and nonprofit, to name a few. There have been so many events and training opportunities that I participated in and coordinated over the years. It is hard to place a few on the paper to share with you; however, let's see where my mind takes me.

In the small town in West Virginia, the site location for negotiations between Israel and Syria to end the fifty-one-year state of war between the Mideast neighbors. Israeli Prime Minister Ehud Barak and Syrian Foreign Minister Farouk al-Sharaa came to the center for a three-day meeting in 2000.

The small town was a buzz as the motorcade, and the president's Marine One helicopter landed at the local college baseball field. White House and state department staff were housed at the center. Foreign leaders were at the local hotel, and the press lodged at the local university.

President Clinton and US Secretary of State Madeleine Albright each met individually with diplomatic teams, led by Israeli Prime Minister Ehud Barak and Syrian Foreign Minister Farouk al-Sharaa. What a time. And a woman coming from extreme poverty in the Appalachian Hills of Virginia was a part of this historical event. As I sit and reminisce, I smile and say, "Wow, I was there to experience this event."

President Jimmy Carter and his staff visited the center several times and spoke to groups. I recall one trip, as he entered the building and proceeded up the ramp, he just stopped and turned around. You could see security becoming alarmed. To his left was our contractor's hotel staff, and folks were gathered from the offices to the front to get a glimpse of the president of the United States. President Carter walked over to the group and chatted for a few minutes; it made everyone's day. I proceeded in front of him to our instructional west building, along with his teams. I stepped back into a small conference room off to the left to allow him to pass. He saw me and stopped and shook my hand. I too was so honored to meet the president. You see, he is only a man; however, his position title brought me to humbleness before him.

Can you imagine when we stand before the Creator of the universe? What will we feel? I can only imagine what that will be like.

It was common for the executive, legislative, and judicial branches to frequent the campus for meetings. I recall a senator from Vermont, his staff, and his loyal assistant, Clara, arriving for annual retreats, and what a welcoming sight. I recall meeting the senator's lovely wife, Louise, and sharing wonderful stories. You see, I am Thelma, and she was Louise. In fun, we remembered the combination in the movie that was made famous in 1991, *Thelma & Louise* movie. She sent me a note, signed by Louise. I still have that wonderful note to help me remember our time together.

I coordinated a Russian sturgeon workshop with our Washington, DC external affairs office and the Russian delegations coming to our facility. I recall researching the culture, customs, and individuals we would host.

The interpreters were scheduled to shadow the Russians and other foreign-speaking individuals who attended the conference to assist the staff in understanding and providing for the needs of these guests. Plans were in place, and signs and menus were converted to their language for their convenience. We set plans in place for the conversion of currency and working with our government contractor's general manager, and we began to put into place the menus for their stay. We translated the meal menus and directions for the campus into their language for easy access.

The room was set up just right. Getting seating and placement of individuals in a strategic meeting is critical for success. What is the best setup for discussion? What level should it be? Is everyone on equal standing, or is one level higher than another? In this meeting, we chose that all individuals were of equal standing.

After months of planning, the day had arrived. One by one, folks from around the world began arriving. The center's director, the assistant to the director, and I were welcoming each other as they arrived. As the evening's opening reception began, we gathered in the reception area, where our food and beverage department delivered wonderful bread that was appropriate for the evening and bread that our Russian group approved. Our Russian friends treated us to Russian caviar. As I recall, the caviar was around $2,000 an ounce. Being a person who had never eaten caviar before, what an eye-opening experience. We gathered around the table where the Russians were serving. We had our drinking glasses in hand and caviar in the other hand. I recall standing next to the assistant to the director, and I was just consumed with the excitement of our guests and my invitation to join them in celebration. Yes, around and around came the drinks. They noticed that my glass was often empty, and here, "another one," the one Russian said. Little did anyone other than the assistant to the director know, I was pouring my drink out when backs were turned. You see, I have never had a drink of this sort in my life!

Soon, one of our Russian friends noticed my hand was empty too. They did not see me pass my caviar off to my friend standing next to me. All of a sudden, my Russian friend and their culture invaded my personal space and shoved caviar into my mouth. "Here," the Russian said. Oh my, yes, I did consume that $2,000 caviar. What an evening it was to remember.

One afternoon, two of the rather large stature men came to visit me at my office. As I knew, I should not shake their hands over a threshold. I attempted to bring them into my space. You take a 115 lb. female and put that person against a three-hundred-pound male, whose space do you think was invaded? Soon I was in the hallway, nose to nose with two wonderful friends. Yes, truly it was fun, however, a bit uncomfortable for an American. The interpreter interpreted all the while.

I don't know if the actual meeting accomplished the goals of all the attendees; however, I am sure all that attended this meeting had a wonderful time and are sharing their story, as they saw it, to their friends, as I am sharing with you.

Another wonderful conference we coordinated was the Native American chiefs' conference. Chiefs from all nations were arriving at our center to meet and discuss issues of concern with the secretary of the interior and other leadership from our nation's capital. Before their arrival, strict security measures were in place for entrance to the campus. We were prepared for any possible public protest, as well as the setup of proper classrooms, foods, and fires to burn around the clock, as is their custom.

I recall, during one segment of the meeting, I was called to the classroom, and one person was banned from attending. The person escorted the individual out into the hallway where I met the individual. We chatted briefly, and I asked him to leave campus. He said no. He indicated, "I will wait here in the break area." I, again and again, asked him to leave. As I continued to use my negotiation skills and encourage him to leave, it was not working. I then said, "Yes, you will leave one way or the other." He again said, "I am not leaving."

I radioed our security law enforcement. And when they arrived, the guest agreed to leave without hesitation.

During this particular conference, I was invited by the Native American chiefs to attend their morning service. What an honor. I was told, when the head chief invites you to their religious service, it is quite special. I should feel honored, which I did. I did not know what to expect. I was given a challenge by the chief to find a place on the campus where the four winds met. *Oh my, where is that?* I thought.

Once I located the site that I would recommend to the chief, our contractor cleared off the space and was ready for their approval. Yes, it was approved by the chiefs. Let me add a side note here. The inspector general asked me, "How did you decide where to place the group?"

I said, "Well, it was difficult. I went outside, wet my finger, and stuck it up in the air to see how the wind blew." There was a hearty laugh coming from his mouth by the time I finished. I indeed did this; however, I knew the best place for the group. The assistant to the director and I worked closely with this group, and all agreed upon the placement.

As the service began that cool morning, the container that smoked was passed around that was to flow from the ground up, and the chief began his prayer. When the chief began talking about me and my character, I was brought to tears. How could the man know me without knowing me? I was so shocked as he talked about me. I thought that was the kind of person I wanted to be; however, I surely have not reached that level. As we began walking back to the classroom that morning, I was so overwhelmed; I spoke with another chief and commented how wonderful and overtaken I was with the chief's comments.

This tall man stopped abruptly and looked me straight in the eye and said, "The chief is very wise. If you were not that person, he would not have said so." Without another word, he opened the door and proceeded down the hallway. You could have knocked me over with a feather. What an experience!

The last day of the conference arrived, and we were saying our goodbyes to all our new friends and buses leaving. The last bus left the campus about thirty minutes earlier before a radio call. "There are two chiefs here in the dining hall." Oh my, and we were now in the middle of a snowstorm, and the roads getting bad. I had no one willing to drive them to the airport. The next best thing was to call one of the buses that had left the center to turn around and come back. The center's employees contacted the bus driver, who was about forty-five minutes out. They turned around and came back to pick up two stray chiefs. What an experience with the nation's Native American chiefs. What an honor to see the dress and culture on campus.

In 2016, the area received forty inches of snow and we had more than three hundred people at the center. The group began to arrive Thursday and Friday as we emptied all of the 226 guest rooms from the previous event and turned the rooms over to accept the next 226 plus onsite guests.

I was welcoming new guests and getting them into rooms as rooms were becoming available as our contractors cleaned the rooms. It began to snow, and it snowed, snowed, and snowed. Our lodge rooms were full, and we now needed places to sleep for food and beverage, hotel reservations, maintenance, land management staff, and me. I asked all the staff to find where they would sleep and coordinate with me at that location. I wanted to know where everyone was sleeping in case a fire or other emergency happened. One by one, the calls were coming in. "I am sleeping on the sofa in Instructional West." "I am sleeping in my office on a borrowed cot." "I brought a blow-up mattress, and I am sleeping second floor of Instructional East," the land manager said. I would be sleeping on the floor in my office. Soon I had the location of all the staff, who were there to serve the guest and assist me.

The snow was piling up. We had young and old in the group, and many challenges facing us and the snow were building up by the hour. The contractors, the coordinator of the event, and I were working and having meetings hour by hour. The land manager was working with folks to clear sidewalks, and I was giving the most important location to clear first. Soon, no one was coming or going from campus. That day, guests were there and there to stay. Going home was not an option. No food trucks were coming in, no buses or cars to pick up people who thought they were going to leave campus. Yes, the main road coming into the campus was shut down.

The campus grounds were being cleared as quickly as possible. We gathered every shovel that was on site, and folks were using everything they could find to clear snow. I was coordinating the movement of the approximate three hundred–plus people and keeping them safe. We had a maintenance tunnel from one of the buildings to another. Maintenance cleared the pathway from the dining hall to the building. They worked on that pathway continually, day and night, to keep it open. We placed signs—"watch your head"—and directed people through the tunnel to another building, where their scheduled training was taking place.

LINES OF LIFE RUN THROUGH THE MOUNTAINS

The day arrived that all were to depart campus: Sunday. Needless to say, no one was going out, and no one was coming in. All buses, flights, pickups were still halted. When the snow finally stopped, we had forty inches of snow. We had many artists in the group, and they went down the paths that were plowed and created snow art on the snow that had not been touched by man. What a beautiful sight it was. Truly talented people shared with everyone, walking around, viewing the creative art. Everyone was having a great time, snowed in at a beautiful facility, sitting around the warm fireplace, snacking on that freshly popped popcorn, and sipping a drink, soft music playing in the background. There was no better place to be snowed in. Little did all of the attendees know what the event coordinator, the contractor's general manager, and I were going through, working out logistics for food, safety, room cleaning, laundry, transportation, flights, local pickups, and more. The food and beverage department was creative with food to ensure there was plenty to eat. We didn't know how many days we would be snowed in, and no trucks were going to make deliveries.

As the days passed, the deputy director who lived rather close to the center came driving in on his four-wheeler. I think he enjoyed the drive and the surprise he gave to me when he arrived. He surprised me by shoveling out my Honda from four feet of snow. He knew, if I got to go home, I would have a job just digging myself out. He took a picture and sent it to me with a "thank you" attached. How wonderful that was, and what a wonderful gesture.

Soon, buses started arriving, and we set up a convoy so if one bus got stranded, others would be behind to assist. By the time the buses were starting to roll off campus, other key personnel were arriving.

After everyone got back to their homes, I began to receive wonderful thank-you notes for such a great event and a wonderful experience. The event coordinator and I had a previous friendship; however, this cemented our ongoing friendship for life. She is and was a wonderful person and coordinator, which I was honored to work with during this and many other events.

I recall many law enforcement training events from a variety of agencies across the United States. I admired their competence, compassion, and no-nonsense approach to every situation. Observing law enforcement in action, performing their annual training with hand-to-hand combat, and working with K9 dogs, tracking drugs and other illegal items were always a wonderful experience. The officers would go for long runs to pass health certification and to meet their annual requirements. The world is a better place when we have law enforcement officers such as these, who are willing to sacrifice and protect us every day.

Special agents sponsored the International Conservation Chiefs Academy (ICCA) to combat illegal wildlife crime. Forty leaders of conservation law enforcement agencies from Africa were to build capacity and collaborate with other leaders from Angola, Botswana, Cameroon, Chad, Republic of Congo, Gabon, Tanzania, Togo, Uganda, Zambia, Rwanda, South Africa, Guinea, Conakry, Kenya, Mozambique for training.

I sponsored an evening event at the local ice cream shop for them. At this establishment, you would take a cup or cone and fill it with the ice cream you wanted, and you would pay by weight at the end of the line. The folks from Botswana had a blast. They just kept filling up cups. I thought there was no way under the sun they could eat that. We sat outside, and they all laughed and scooped up the ice cream, which some had never eaten before. It was a sight to see, and for me to be part of this was an incredible experience seeing grown men look like kids in a candy store. I am sure it was something they will never forget. There are so many stories I could share; however, I should move on.

When I was hired by the DOI, I lived four hours away from the office. I was not able to relocate closer to the job due to family commitments and finances. So what was I to do? The daily travel would be over mountainous terrain and two-lane roads for most of the trip. I would be up and out of the house by 3:00 a.m. and arrive at work by 7:30 a.m. five days a week, a forty-hour workweek. I would return home around 8:30 p.m. Could I do this? Could I accept this job? The answer was a resounding "yes, I can do this." You see, I had two foster children and a husband at home to care for, so staying near the job was not an option.

I was off to bed by midnight and back up by 3:00 a.m. across the mountains, where intense fog, snow, and ice were common. Occasionally I would spend the night with our daughter in Towson, Maryland, if I had someone at home to care for our foster children for the night.

I was in *Ripley's Believe it or Not*, August 1995, for the longest daily commute over mountain terrain. What a trip each day. Sometimes I wonder how I did it, even during blizzards in the 1990s. During the 1996 blizzard, I went to work each day, and each day the facility was closed until Friday because of the thirty-eight-inch snowstorm.

Thursday night, I received a call from the project leader, who was amazed that I had been at the office all week. He gave me an administrative day off and said, "Do not show up tomorrow." I remember it like it was yesterday. Some of the staff came to me later, concerned that I would get to work, and they lived down the street and could not come to work. During these times, office attendance improved greatly.

I have been so blessed—a young woman coming from the Appalachian coalfields of Virginia and from a family in poverty, to be able to gain such a position and responsibilities that I was entrusted with is an awesome feeling. If it had not been for support from my lifelong partner and husband, I would not have been able to be this giving person to so many people. He sacrificed our time together for my career. Many evenings I would walk in the door very late. He was always there to take my coat, get me a glass of tea, take my shoes off, and say, "Welcome home. I missed you."

We have three very successful children, two work for the Department of Justice, and one worked for the US Geological Survey and now is employed by the Army Corps of Engineers. We raised two foster children: one who works in the medical field, and the other has severe cerebral palsy and could never work. My husband and I have six grandchildren and four great-granddaughters. In addition, our foster daughter has three children, and with our children's blended families, we can add about a dozen more to our family tree. We raised adults, and our children raised adults. My husband and I reap those benefits every day. The children that are old enough have and will continue to contribute to society, just as I feel I have.

I am number eight among my mother's births. I recall living in the Inman camp. My sister and I were allowed to practice our gymnastics, including our backbends, only after all of the chores were completed.

While in the yard, practicing our gymnastics, we thought we were going to be the greatest gymnasts ever. We didn't know what we were talking about or how we were going to be the greatest. I suppose we had fun dreaming of being great gymnasts someday. Up to a few short years ago, in our senior years, she and I could still do a complete backbend and return.

Moving to Maryland from the small community in Virginia was a shock to me. Mother said I did not adapt well. I hooked school and sat outside in the alley all day and pretended I went to school until the school wondered where I was. I hated the city, the house, and the people who laughed at me for my Southern accent. I also felt that the teacher hated me. She had me sit next to a girl that no one wanted to be around; she smelled from not bathing. Being new to the city, I just thought no one liked me. I recall, after many days of being laughed at and picked on, which today we call bullying, I put a stop to it.

Remember, I came from the country and a large family where you fought with your fist sometimes, even though Mother disagreed with that. We were going up the final flight of stairs at school, and two girls behind me were laughing at me and making fun of my speech. We got close to the top. I had enough. I turned around with my fist in the air, and I was going to grab girl number one and fist her. Immediately, things turned in my direction. The girls backed off, and from that day in the fourth grade until graduation, neither girl ever said a word to me again. As you can gather, we never became friends!

I was the only child from a family of ten who graduated from high school and attended any formal training and college. Many of our children, grandchildren, nieces, and nephews have gone on to higher education with masters and doctorate degrees, and some also own their businesses. All of them make our family proud.

The legacy of a family from the coalfield of Southwest Virginia in the Appalachian hills will be known for generations to come through the children, grandchildren, great-grandchildren, and great-great-grandchildren who will follow in their ancestor's footsteps. They will contribute to this world with all their skills, talents, education, and determination that has flown from the bloodline of a short four-foot-eleven-inch-tall woman and a five-foot-eleven-inch-tall man dressed in his tailor-made suit and the Stetson hat, with his little bride and lifelong partner standing, holding on to him for their lifetime.

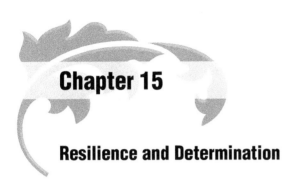

Chapter 15

Resilience and Determination

Resilience is the capacity to withstand or to recover quickly from difficulties; toughness (*Webster*).

Determination is firmness of purpose; resoluteness (*Webster*).

This family of ten faced their challenges and overcame them with success. I would guess our family's struggles may be similar to your family's challenges. We were able to overcome our challenges, and I believe you can too, and you can make an even greater difference in this life than we did. Every person you meet, in person or online, you can make a difference in their life. You never know what a person is going through. They may laugh, as my sister did many times, and yet be frail, broken, and alone.

My mother, pregnant every two years, spoke often about the struggles she went through as a woman. She had nine of the children at home and child number 10 in the hospital. She had children in diapers for twenty years. There were no disposable diapers. There were cloth diapers that you rinsed out and then scrubbed the diapers on the scrub board and hung them up to dry. They were not store-bought diapers; they were old towels or clothes cut into squares for diapers. She breastfed all of the children; it was the thing to do, and she also saved money. Mother said, when the second child was born, she had no breast milk. It dried up, and there was no money to buy milk. Mother said, her sister, who had a baby at the same time, breastfed my second brother until he was old enough to eat food. Mother said he would have died if it had not been for her sister and his aunt breastfeeding him.

Mother said it wasn't that she wanted to plant a garden, can the food, wash clothes on a scrub board, cut hair, cook, or make our clothes; she just had no choice. There was no protection for the woman to stop pregnancies. She said, each month, when she did not get her cycle, her heart would ache. She knew how hard it was going to be for her and the child. Little did she have to offer the child.

When Mother had cotton material or grain sacks from items she purchased at the store, she would make some new clothes for us. She did not use a pattern. She would take our measurements—width, length, and circumference—place the material on the table or the floor, and start cutting. In a little while, you would hear her call your name when she pinned the shirt, skirt, or dress around your body. Then back to the treadle sewing machine, she would go. Again, in a little while, your name would be called again, and we did this as many times as she needed us to do. Once it was all done, then the hemming would start. She never hemmed on the machine; it was by hand. And as we got older, she had us hem the article of clothing. Mother said we must learn to sew since we needed this skill to care for our family. I liked to watch her sew, and I learned to sew from her. I don't remember if any other child liked to sew in those days. Later in life, my sister, child number 5, and Mother would sew and make quilts.

Mother had to be creative with everything she did to feed and clothe us. Not only did she sew, but she also made things we did not have, like whipped butter.

Mother would place heavy cream and salt into a quart jar and have us shake, shake, and shake it until it became butter. I can't remember what else she placed in the jar if anything. All of us children remember sitting on the porch in the swing and shaking the jar to create whipped butter.

As we sat on the swing, Father would teach us the kind of car that would go up the road. His words, "That's a Studebaker. That's a Pontiac," and so on. It was said, my baby brother, child number 10, knew just about every type of car at a very young age.

Father would sit on the swing and tell us stories. One story he shared was that he was digging coal far back into the mines, and he found the sole of a shoe embedded deep into the coal. He believed it was so deep in the mine that it must have come from the day of the flood in Noah's time of the Bible. He had that sole for a long time. I have wondered many times what he did with that sole of the shoe. I wish I could remember.

In the evenings, after dinner and if the family was not working in the garden, they were sitting on the porch, letting the house cool off before bedtime or visiting the neighbor down the road.

When Mother and Father moved down into the community, Mother had the greatest friend ever, the next-door neighbor. She had seven boys and one girl. Today, on Facebook, I have connected with the family. Four of them are still alive, and they are living in Maryland. Mother spoke so highly of the family and had special memories of them.

One thing is for sure, as we grew up in the country, we always went to church on Sunday at the little white Baptist Church upon the hill. Father would pray with one knee on the floor and the other holding his Stetson hat.

The outhouse (toilet) was out at the back of the church. The children went to the outhouse, and coming back we stopped and looked into the window, where the congregation was washing the feet of others, as the Bible speaks of. We thought this was so funny, and Mother saw us and pointing her little bony finger at us. We knew we were in trouble, and we would be corrected. That was the last time we ever did that.

Back in those days, the church was full of people, and they would go down to the river and have baptism services. It seemed like the whole town celebrated this important day with you.

As some of the children were working, Father was able to purchase his very first car. It was a 1929 Ford Model A. It was said, all of us would not fit into the car at one time. We took turns going to town on the trip next week or next month. Occasionally, while in town, Mother would purchase a loaf of store-bought bread. We thought it was wonderful and such a special treat. Can you imagine a piece of bread instead of a piece of pie was a treat?

When I was in the seventh grade of school, my girlfriends wanted to begin smoking, so we made a pack that each week, one of us would buy the cigarettes. We were only into this pack a couple of weeks when I stood up for myself and said no more.

It was my turn to purchase the cigarettes, and I did not have any money. I knew my father had some antique, old money in a small container in the house. I took the money, maybe a quarter, to purchase the cigarettes, and that's when I decided I would not smoke anymore. I stole from my father. And if I would get money, I wanted to spend it on potato chips and a Coke. Later in life, after I was married, I visited one of my old friends, and she was a chain-smoker at that time. She said she wished a thousand times she had quit when I did.

Just remember, our decision when we are young will follow us forever. Rethink the decision you are about to make!

By now you may be asking, what happened to the children number four through seven? I did not forget them throughout these pages. Their challenges were great, and their successes are even greater.

Child number 7, Ruth Ann (January 25, 1945), worked hard all her life and raised three children on her own. You see, she too had a very difficult life, and her children kept her going. She has two boys, born on the same day, one year apart. She has one beautiful daughter. All of them live in South Carolina.

In 1979, when the Baltimore Convention Center opened, she was one of the first employees. She worked there until her retirement in 2009.

See recalls the first contractor that acquired the contract at the Baltimore Convention Center had the contract for four years, then lost the contract. Then fifteen years later, they acquired the contract again. She recalls the manager, her boss, whom she began under in 1979, was also the boss when they regained the contract after fifteen years. The boss remembered my sister. She said the Lord always gave her good bosses who cared for her and supported her during very difficult times of her life.

She recalls many events that she and her coworkers were a part of, setting the tables for breakfast, lunch, and dinner for up to five thousand people at an event. She worked long hours to have finances to care for her family. The company trusted and respected her, and she in turn trusted and respected them. She trusted in the Lord and said the Lord always provided her with protection, security, a babysitter, and food on the table when she was in desperate situations. She said the Lord had a plan for her life.

When she applied for Social Security, she discovered her husband didn't work and had not paid into Social Security. He was in and out of prison most of their married life. You may ask, why didn't she leave him? I, too, asked that question. She said, "I always loved him, and I made a vow when I married him, until death do us part, and I kept my promise to him and God." He passed away on April 14, 1989.

Today, she enjoys retirement and her small beautiful home, enjoying her children and grandchildren. She said, "In retirement, the Lord has blessed and provided for me."

Yes, the Lord truly had a plan for her life, as he has a plan for your life. She has given to every person that has come across her path. She has cared for many until they left this earth, asking nothing of them. Her life was filled with many mistakes, bad decisions, lots of pain, hurt, and disappointments, yet she is a survivor of a life of drugs, alcohol, verbal, and physical abuse from her husband and became a strong, powerful, successful, and determined woman.

You won't hear her complain. If you talk to her, within a few minutes, you will hear how good the Lord is to her. She is and has been an angel sent to this earth. She cared for her mother, who was home on her deathbed. Mother was told, within three days, she would be dead. I recall her calling me and saying that was what the doctor said. She said, "I don't know. I feel good, just tired." One by one, each child arrived in South Carolina, and we watched our mother's health deteriorate hour by hour. On the third day, she left this world. Father had a ministroke weeks before Mother became ill. He did not fully understand what was happening. Mother and Father were staying with child number 6, our sister, Nell, and her family at that time. Mother did not let go of this life until our eldest brother finally arrived in South Carolina. Shortly after he arrived, and he gave Mother one red rose, then she left this world with her children, grandchildren, and husband by her side.

I left my mother's room around 6:00 p.m. that evening, and I did not go back into the room. Mother passed away around 3:00 a.m. Her granddaughter, who was a registered nurse, came into the room and disconnected the equipment attached to her. The next day, Father kept asking when she would be coming back home from the hospital. I shared with him she wasn't coming home, and to this day, I remember the look of brokenness on his face that I will never forget. He gradually began to give up on life himself, and thirteen months later, in February, he left this world too.

You see, I could never measure up to the jobs that other members of the family have done and accomplished. I will continue trying to make a difference to someone. Everyone has the responsibility to make this world a better place and leave this world better than when we began. I hope you and I have accomplished or will accomplish this. I believe my siblings, three brothers and one sister, and their families will continue this work until life is no more for the five on this earth.

Two in our family had cancer: my brother Hubert, child number 4, and my sister Nell, child number 6.

Around 1995, I received a call at work from my brother, who began to tell me of his throat cancer diagnosis story. I remember I got so angry. He was a chain-smoker, and I always fussed with him since I hated cigarette smoke. I remember telling him, "You got what you deserved," in my moment of anger. I was so wrong, and I apologized to him many times over. He never held it against me.

Of course, no one should get cancer. He managed it quite well and lived probably twenty-five years after his diagnosis. He was a great warrior, provided for a large family of nine, and was known by everyone as the candy man. He made his fudge candy to a level of perfection that few can reach. He has many grandchildren, great-grandchildren, and four children alive today, three boys and one girl.

If you, who read this, have cancer, I can relate to your illness, as we struggled, as we watched our brother and sister struggle. They tried to find something in life to focus on. Hubert loved his sports teams and submerged himself in those players and games. You would not hear him complain. He loved life, even when he was so sick, and he never lost his faith or smile. You hang in there, "Whether we live, we live unto the Lord, or if we die we die unto the Lord" (Romans 14:8 KJV).

My sister, child number 6, Glacy Nell (December 12, 1942), had skin cancer on her back and kept it a secret for many years. Her husband, children, brothers, and sisters did not know about it until it was at a critical stage. Her daughter, who was a registered nurse and my angel sister, Ruth, cared for her for two hard years until she passed away at home with her husband and family by her side. Nell was the feistiest child Mother had. She was kind and good, but if you crossed her or lied to her, she had no problem cursing you out without any reservation and then make a cake or pie and bring it to you!

For many years, she devoted herself to our parents. If our parents wanted to go somewhere or wanted an item, she saw that they got it. She brought them into her home to live and care for them until their death. Nursing homes were out of the question for her parents. Mother passed away in her home. Nell had two children, one boy and one girl, and five beautiful grandchildren, whom she loved dearly, at the time of her death.

My brother, Eddie Lee (January 18, 1941) was the fifth child born in our family. Mother spoke of Lee getting sick when he was very young and running a very high temperature, and with no way to transport him to the doctor or hospital, Mother became the doctor. She said she used all of the home remedies, put Vicks salve on his little body and sat for three days in front of the fireplace, rocking him while wrapped in blankets until his fever broke. Mother said, after this, he always seems to have some emotional problem. He always appeared very nervous and was agitated easily. The other children saw he had some newfound fears, and they used them to scare him, as young kids will do. It was said his brothers would go outside at night, place sheets over their bodies, and pretend they were ghosts. Lee was terrified of the ghost that lived on the property.

In his adult life, he had a great personality, and finding and keeping a job was easy for him. He later married a beautiful woman from our church. In a short time, they had four children, two boys and two girls. Their marriage struggled to succeed over the next few years. The day came, and they divorced. My brother struggled with letting go and began to drink pretty heavily. My mother was always on to him to get his act together. It was more difficult than we realized.

Time passed, and he moved around from state to state, avoiding paying child support, only thinking of himself for a few years, and struggling to become the person he was when he was younger. Again, he chose the road to the left for many years, as did my sister you have read about. In the meantime, his ex-wife was raising those beautiful children. Her parents were a great help to her, and my sister and I were close friends too since we went to church together, years before my brother met his wife.

Time passed, and Lee married a second time in Cincinnati, Ohio. During this second marriage, he began paying back the state of Maryland all child support that he owed until it was all paid.

He met his obligation to the state. It was more difficult to call back all of the years he had without his children. As the years passed, he built a better relationship with his sons and daughters.

Time waits for no one, so he doesn't have a lot of years to show them how much he loves them. He often would tell his sister Ruth, who cared for him until the day he passed, that he loved his kids and was proud of them. My brother died of Parkinson's disease.

I share these stories with you since I realize you may have some of the same challenges in your life, your family, and your children. Life is like a puzzle; you have added pieces all your life, and you have been making a picture. What will that picture look like at the end of the road, the end of your life? It will be your creation. You and I can't change the past; however, we can still make amends for mistakes, even upon our deathbed. We must not allow opportunities to pass us by. Don't let pride or selfishness rule our lives anymore. You and I are more than conquerors through Christ Jesus our Lord (Romans 8:31 KJV).

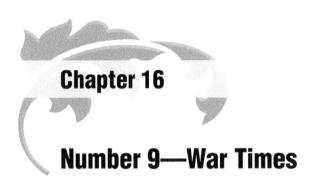

Chapter 16

Number 9—War Times

Child number 9, Larry Garland (June 12, 1949), was a fighter in his younger life. When he got mad, the fists would fly, and they flew often. His fighting career was in school and at home with his siblings. He was tough and strong as a young child.

Like all Mother's children, Larry had a job to do at home. While living in Virginia, his major job was to carry water. He remembers carrying water from the spring to the house and getting to the house, half of the water was gone. So back to the spring again and again. There was no need to complain; it would go unnoticed.

Larry recalls a Christmas play he participated in. He had a small verse to memorize and recite. And for participating, his reward would be a bag of oranges. He wanted the oranges, and even though he was shy, he agreed to be in the play. On the night of the production, he stood on the stage with stage fright, looked at the audience, and off the stage he ran, grabbing his bag of oranges!

Larry has little memory of the old home place, where he lived in his young years.

Larry was a fixer and builder. If you need something repaired, call Larry. If you need something designed and built, call Larry. His experience working with wood extends a lifetime. He is known to create masterpieces with wood. You think it, he can build it. It is a God-given talent, which few possess.

He was always building and working with wood even at a young age. He recalls telling his mother he could not find a rock to use as a hammer while living in the city. If he could find wood, it was going to be made into something. He loved creating things. With few toys, he thought he would just build his own. He recalls he wanted a wagon, and his mother and father did not have the finances to purchase one. You guessed it. He decided to build himself a wagon, and build a wagon he did.

He loved to roller-skate on borrowed skates; we had none of our own. With street chalk, he drew hopscotch games on the sidewalk and enjoyed the challenge with other players. He loved running the street and playing hide-and-seek with all the kids in the neighborhood. It was safe in those days in the city. He played late into the night, and no one cared if the children were still on the streets; no one in the neighborhood thought or feared getting shot as people do today.

He was not the most studious student. He recalls not liking school and once even hooked school, and he surely got in trouble with his mother. He was corrected, and he never did that again. He recalls the sixth-grade teacher knocking on our house door to ask questions or report he was not in school, fighting in school, or bringing Bowie knives to school for show-and-tell. The knives did not belong to him and should have never taken them out of the house. Again, he was corrected for this, and it never happened again.

Children do not realize the dangers of doing things like this. Most of the time, young children act innocently since their brains are not fully developed at such an early stage in life.

With all of the ten children, Mother would assign each child a child to be responsible for.

Larry was assigned to me, Thelma. Everywhere I went, Larry went, and where Larry went, I went. We did not like these arrangements; however, that was the way it was in our family. Even as a child, we were taught to love our God, protect one another, love our siblings, and work hard to succeed.

The day came, and Larry was no more a child. It seemed he became a man overnight. He put away the little boy's toys and fighting with his siblings and took on country patriotism. He desired to go into the military. Mother was reluctant to agree since it was not a time of peace but war. Mother vividly recalled years earlier two of her other children were in the military and how she worried and prayed for them continually. After much contemplation and discussion with Father, they agreed; Larry won the battle with Mother and Father.

Larry was seventeen years of age. He was underage, and one of his parents signed and gave permission for him to join the military. His father had no education and could not read or write; his mother would sign.

He joined the army in 1966, just as the conflict in Vietnam was raging. The conflict was active from November 1, 1955, until the fall of Saigon on April 30, 1975. It formally began under the presidency of Dwight D. Eisenhower and ran throughout the John F. Kennedy's, Lyndon Johnson's, Gerald Ford's, and Richard Nixon's presidency. President Nixon signed a peace treaty, agreeing to end the war in 1973 with Vietnam and Southeast Asia.

Larry and many of his friends went to Fort Bragg, North Carolina, for what was called boot camp, and then on to Fort Dix, New Jersey, for more training. They were trained in many areas of urban and jungle warfare, different types of gunnery, and most importantly, how to survive a battle. For urban warfare, small man-created villages were built, and soldiers would meander throughout the village and roads, looking for the enemy or booby traps.

It was a make-believe town with cutouts for people. One would pop up, and the soldier reacted. There was training, training, and more training, where your actions became second nature, so when you would be in a real battle, you wouldn't hesitate; you would just react. Hesitating could get you killed, and quickly reacting would save your life.

Jungle warfare training was much different from urban warfare. The environment in the jungle was fog, rain, mud, brush, bushes, vines, thick underbrush, and getting acclimated to high temperature, humidity, typhoons, rain, and being ready for the monsoon season. You quickly learned if you were in gullies, and rain came. You could quickly be washed away if you did not wrap your legs around a tree truck to keep from sliding down the mountain with the mud. The soldiers needed and received training on how to react during a typhoon. On the beach at Camp Eagle, you could spread full eagle and lean into a typhoon, and it was like flying.

After basic training, while in New Jersey, he was able to go home, which was to Baltimore, Maryland. He left home as a young boy and came home on furlough as a man. Seeing Larry dressed in his uniform and that clean-shaven, short haircut made his very appearance, demanding respect as a soldier. What a day of great pride for his parents and siblings. I remember how proud they were of their boy who overnight became a man.

Larry always took great pride in the military and wanted to be a good soldier, a good representative of the American people and the United States of America. He wanted to live up to the army slogan: "Be all you can be."

It was easy for him to look sharp in the military. He recalls how he emulated successfully military personnel. He felt proud when he would go for morning formation for inspection. He would walk stiff legged down the stairs so his pant legs would not wrinkle. He had all his uniforms tailored so they were perfect. The local tailor sewed the seams into the shirts and pants and sewed his patches onto the uniform with perfection. His boots were spit shined and would shine like clear glass. He polished his boots every chance he got. He would wrap them individually and store them in his locker so they would be perfect when he put them on for inspection.

He looked the part and dressed the part always, especially during the inspection.

When the sergeant would ask, "What's your basic load on an M14? Who is the speaker of the house and what is your congressman's name?" "Who is your senator?" "What is your carry load?"

Larry knew all the answers to questions the sergeant would ask. Larry was eager to learn everything he could learn to "be the best you could be." He was proud and would be nothing less than a good soldier.

If you were the colonel's orderly, you got the day off if you were called out and knew the answers to all of the questions the sergeant would ask. If you thought you looked better than another person selected, you could challenge it. Every time they would fall out, the men would see Larry's name on the guard roster, and they would say, "I will pay you $25 if you pull night duty for me. "Look the part, dress the part, and know all the answers to questions the first sergeant would ask if anyone could get the day off. That was easy for me," he said.

The day arrived, and he would leave his beloved United States of America and head to foreign lands to defend the country he loved. Young, invincible, and full of excitement and yet with some anxiousness for the unknown—he boarded the plane with other new soldiers and headed to Germany.

While in Germany, the soldiers trained at a center that was classified as a "center of training excellence." It was a strange feeling that everyone needed to overcome since they were training where Adolph Hitler trained his military. Adolph Hitler's men murdered over six million Jews.

This training site had live fire and maneuver ranges. You could acquire qualifications that range from tanks, M16 rifle, artillery, and small arms and train in air support and others. It is said that many organizations have trained at the sites. Patton's army trained here. Westmoreland's army trained here. Col. Powell's army trained here. Hitler and Mussolini were here too. The king of rock and roll and singer Elvis Presley had been there too (Wikipedia).

As I was told, men came and went at the German base: men completing missions in Vietnam, men going to Vietnam. It was a camp on the move.

In Germany, before he changed his MOS (military operation specialist), he was the field wireman, which was the lowest in the military ranking system. He was a private. Being a low man on the totem pole, he would pull a lot of KP and guard duty. KP duty means kitchen police or kitchen patrol work under the kitchen staff assigned to junior US enlisted military personnel. Performing his job was easy for him. He was young and strong. He could climb those telephone poles and hang telephone wires in seconds. While working in communication, he learned to operate various communication equipment, learning to code and decode messages that were received and sent. He also operated the army radio and switchboard equipment. Even though these jobs and skills were critical, especially in times of war, he still longed for more.

Larry was proud to be in a convoy of one hundred trucks, even though he was driving the last truck. You see, when you are inexperienced, the last thing the military wants is you to be in the front of the line, holding up everyone. However, by the time he left Germany, he was in a convoy of one hundred trucks, and he was driving the first truck.

Larry changed his MOS to truck driver. At home, Father did not have a car, so Larry had no experience driving, and he only had a motorcycle license, no driver's license. However, there was another young man in his unit who came from a farm and could drive anything. The platoon sergeant said, "Get him to teach you to drive." Larry said, "I learned to drive and took my driving test in the army's five-ton dump truck." There were one hundred questions on the test, and all the European signs and international road signs, you needed to know. He passed with flying colors. "Boy was it fun driving a truck as my first vehicle. Only in the army could I do this!"

He didn't want to stay in one place. He was young, full of energy, and felt he was invincible. He wanted to see the world and fight for his country.

As he stayed in Germany longer and longer, soldiers came and went to and from Vietnam. Over time, he was the longest soldier at the base. "I think everyone, including the colonel and everyone, had left. Over time, new soldiers were coming." Larry became the senior member at the base. He got all the benefits in picking and choosing where he wanted to go and what he wanted to do. He wanted to be the best he could be, and he was eager to learn everything that was expected of him and more.

Every month, they had a full practice alert. At times, it was 2:00 a.m. They would be fully prepared and ready for battle if an invasion occurred from unlikely Russia. They would get all the equipment and load their demo truck with the ammunition and any other items needed in case of an invasion. There were no rules, no speed limits. It was really exciting for a seventeen-year-old man. It was not exciting when it was a real battle. Those real battles were memories all of the soldiers wanted to forget.

The military was constantly training the men in all areas of preparedness. The soldiers were to be prepared for anything that could occur at any time. Their training occurred during the daytime and during the nighttime hours. The soldiers were aware the enemy could attack at any time, and the soldiers would be prepared, day or night.

The soldiers would build floating bridges. The soldiers had twenty-four hours to build the bridge over the Rhine. Once finished, the tank division would drive across the bridge as a test for durability. Then the soldiers would take it down. They built the Bailey Bridges, which is a type of portable, pre-fabricated truss bridge. Another bridge they built was a hundred-foot bridge that you could roll on rollers, or eighty-five guys could roll it with a winch or completely roll it by hand. On the front end, it had a watch post stuck up on the angle and counterweight. It would roll out over the bridge span and come and sit down where it was supposed to. They would drive trucks across the bridge to check for durability, and the men would take them back down. This was training in case of a real need for bridge crossings. He loved the activities and challenges that he faced and overcame. He was an overachiever. He would say, "Give me more to do!"

Larry was on furlough for two weeks, and he looked forward to going home. After the visit, he boarded a plane to Fort Lewis, Washington, for two weeks of training on jungle warfare. Larry said, "We were up north in Washington State in January for jungle training, and it was in January and fourteen degrees, and they were teaching us how to fight jungle warfare. The soldiers thought that was funny." The training was complex and intense.

In Germany, he used the M14 rifle. In Vietnam, he used the M16 rifle. He became an expert with both rifles. Larry was ready to go to the next assignment and fight alongside his fellow soldiers.

He worked hard at every job, learned all he could learn, and trained as much as possible. He was dedicated to the army, his comrades, and the American people, whom he represented.

Larry knew this was not a vacation. He knew, even though he visited many places while in the military and on leave. He saw lives being lost every day. Often, the runways of the airstrip were scattered with fallen soldiers lying, waiting for transport back home to their loved ones. The pain was and is still severe. He said, "You see it changes you. You had no choice but to look for some good and go on."

Several of his hometown friends were already in Vietnam, and he felt it was his duty to be there too. One of his childhood friends had reenlisted for another six months. And when he returned to Vietnam, he was killed thirteen days after arriving in Vietnam.

The men and women of the US military defend our liberties all around the world every day, so we, as citizens, don't have to fight the enemy in our front yard.

Leaving Saigon and going to Cam Ranh Bay, an inlet of the South China Sea, they boarded a C-130 plane, a cargo plane. There were straps across the whole plane, holding the soldiers in place. They were sleeping on their duffel bag. Cam Ranh Bay was the headquarters of the 101st Airborne Brigade. Larry was part of the 101st Brigade, which is highly respected, feared, and called upon when men and women are needed in Vietnam and other places around the world.

The men went to Cam Ranh Bay, where it was hot, to get used to the climate and temperature. Since the temperature in Vietnam is 110 to 120 each day during the summer season. He said, "They needed to acclimate themselves to that climate that they would be enduring."

Not only were the temperatures going to be high in Vietnam, but they would also be facing the Monsoon wet and dry seasons. During one rainy season, Vietnam received fifty-seven inches of rain in one week. At their Camp Eagle, they received twenty-nine and a half inches of rain in seven days.

As he trained and passed all necessary trainings, he was prepared to fight, if necessary. As he recalls, he was assigned to the 101st. Airborne Division, 9th Engineering Battalion. Research says, there were about 900 engineers and 15,000 foot soldiers in his division. The 101st Airborne Division (air assault) is the only air assault division of the United States Army.

Nicknamed the Screaming Eagles, the 101st has consistently distinguished itself by demonstrating the highest standards of military professionalism since its activation one minute after midnight, August 16, 1942.

On August 19 of that year, the first commander promised his recruits that although the new division had no history, it would soon have a rendezvous with destiny. As a division, the 101st has never failed that prophecy.

The 101st is recognized for its unmatched air assault capability, its ability to execute any combat or contingency mission anywhere in the world, and is still proving as tomorrow's division in today's army.

Larry's platoon leaving, flew north to Camp Eagle and the headquarters of the 101st Airborne. On February 1, 1972, Camp Eagle was turned over to the ARVN (Army of Republic Vietnam). The base is abandoned and turned over to farmland, light industry, and housing. Peaceful farmland now, however, the memories of all those who fought and many who died there will never be forgotten (Wikipedia).

While at Camp Eagle, Larry received his orders and was assigned to the Charlie Company. That was LZ Sally (landing zone), which was on another side of the city of Hue. In 1968, this was where the big battle was, and many men on both sides had fallen. The fighting was intense. Larry recalled, "My squad was fogged in on a firebase, where they had been, and their two helicopters crashed, trying to get to the men to get them supplies, food, and ammunition. Men were stuck on this hilltop. The first sergeant sent Larry back to Camp Eagle, where the Green Berets were training men how to repel out of helicopters. At this time, the 101st Airborne was transitioning to airmobile.

"When I reached E-5, they trained me to repel off a tower and hook it up. I was trained to train the platoon." Larry then showed the platoon how to tie up a rope. And after all were rescued, the team all had to go back for official training and jump the one-hundred-foot tower—one side was free fall, and one side was repelled down the wall—slide down ten to fifteen feet, kick off the wall, and go down another ten to fifteen feet until you reach the bottom.

Larry wanted to advance, and he took every opportunity that was afforded to him to gain grades from a private up to E-5. You would be promoted if you did each job well. Larry was taking advantage of every opportunity that came by and changing his MOS (military operation specialist) so he would and could advance in the military. When he entered the service, Larry, a private, ended his military career as an E-5.

Larry gained the status of E-5 and became a demolition specialist. Becoming a demolition specialist was right up his alley, so to speak. As a youngster, he loved to take things apart to see what it was made of. If the toy could be destroyed, he destroyed it.

At that time, a lot of the demolition work was mathematics. In the 1960s, they did not have the equipment to do all of the calculations and formulas. You needed to be good at mathematics in all aspects of building and creating bridges and anything you would come across. You did all the calculations and formulas. There were no computers to do the calculations for you.

Larry said, "Just think, being eighteen to nineteen years old, carrying around explosives and blowing up things every day. How much fun was that? And you think you are invincible? I was living a dream."

However, there were times when we became frightened. In the darkness of the night, tall grasses and bushes, we would shoot flares into the air to give us some light as we fired our weapons into the brush in all directions at the enemy. It was just what we had to do to survive.

Larry's basic job was to go into the jungle with one or two other guys, repelled out, and blow down trees, and hopefully, the ground infantry could go in for a battle with the enemy.

Sometimes you would get hung up in the trees, and the helicopter would pull you back out of the trees and lower you back down. Sometimes the jump was from forty to fifty feet up, sometimes just at tree top level. Sometimes five to six feet from the ground, and you just jumped to the ground. You carried everything you needed, including your food and water. Once a week, you were resupplied on the same day. Often, men were sent to look for streams of water. When they located a stream, they would fill containers and place an iodine tablet into the water for purification. They would land on a hill somewhere where some men would go into the woods to run the enemy out.

The men needed to make it to the rice patties before dark, where the helicopter would take them out.

This was an everyday event. The army did not want you in the jungle beyond twenty-nine days. If you were there for thirty days, you received your combat infantry badge (CIB). "I was there twenty-nine days. I was taken out for one day and sent back. I did not receive the CIB. I received an infantry badge."

When he was being trained for helicopter jumping, the soldiers would board the helicopter with six to eight men. Four would hook up on the rope, two in front and two in the back. One in front would jump, then one in the back. You would have at least ten feet of rope on the floor.

When you jumped out of the plane backward, the excess rope would keep you from going under the helicopter.

When the marines contacted the 101st Airborne and asked if they could do a rescue mission, their sergeant volunteered their company for this mission, as he often offered up their services. The marine military helicopter, often called the jolly Green Giant, with several soldiers on board, had lost contact and suspected it went down on the hilltop in heavy brush. Larry had only two months left of his enlistment, and he would be going home. His thoughts: *Oh, how I wondered, home or another critical mission?*

His team was directed to find the helicopter and rescue those on board. It was during the monsoon season, often mud, drizzling rain, hot, humid, foggy conditions while keeping a keen eye out for the enemy. The team began their search and repelled into the zone to retrieve the men. Remaining on guard and encountering hostel fire, his unit of men must find the wreckage quickly and get the men out of the area. Six soldiers with twenty foot soldiers and six engineers repelled in on the hilltop, where it was suspected the helicopter had crashed. When the men repelled in, there was no sign of the wreckage. For the next four or five hours in the fog and drizzling rain, the men went down the muddy steep hillside, searching and always watching for the enemy.

After several hours, they found the helicopter. All the guns were stripped off by the enemy, and all the men were deceased. The team of men would wrap the bodies of their fallen brothers and send them up to the helicopter on the rollers, while other helicopters would come in to take his team out. Without losing any more men, they hope to get out of the jungle brush before nightfall, along with their deceased army brothers.

The evening was quickly approaching, and they needed to get out of this valley as soon as possible. Because of the trees and brush, the helicopters could not make the pickup. He and his commander began setting C-4 explosives for clearance for the helicopter to come in.

When the charges would be set, they would quickly climb up the mountain as quickly as possible before the charge went off. As they climbed the hill, they came across a poisonous bamboo viper, a little green snake, the first snake they had seen while in Vietnam. You could not stop, keep climbing before the blast. You could never get far enough away from the blast. All was going well, except for one big tree, standing about one hundred yards down the mountain. It was a tall tree, about six feet in diameter, and they put all the explosives they had into this tree. They had about fifteen minutes to climb back up that steep mountain, away from the blast. When the blast was over, they looked back, and there the tree was still standing, weaving back and forth in the drizzling rain and fog. The plane could not get to them with the tree there. Oh, the thoughts on their minds: *Are we going to be stranded for the night?* They set off all the charges they had. They heard a cracking sound, and the tree began to fall. What an incredible sight to see. For this search and rescue mission, Larry was awarded the Bronze Star for bravery.

The platoon was to protect the base and bridges. Larry's main job was to blow bridges or roads to protect the company from invasion or danger. They would create craters in the road with explosives so the enemy would have trouble reaching the men.

Larry's company was sent to the TET offensive attack on Tan Son Nhut Air Base in 1968. Many soldiers were lost in this battle. At this time, it was the Republic of Vietnam Air Force (RVNAF) facility. It was located near the city of Saigon in Southern Vietnam.

The United States used it as a major base during the Vietnam War (1959–1975), stationing the army, Air Force, Navy, and Marine units there. Following the Fall of Saigon, it was taken over as a Vietnam People's Air Force (VPAF) facility and remains in use today (Wikipedia).

The battle on Tan Son Nhut Air Base was a day that will never be forgotten. These are battles that play over and over in the young soldiers' lives and have led over into their middle and senior years. When they think back to this day, it is as real and live as it was on that horrible day in 1968. The day will live forever, and forever is a very long time.

The airplane Larry was on was coming in for the landing, and the enemy was dropping NAPALM bombs on the runway. The officers said, "When we lay the plane down, and the doors open, run a straight line into the bunkers." Larry and his platoon were under heavy fire, and men were falling on every side. Larry said it was probably the worst day his company had experienced. He struggles to talk about this day, even today. It has been a day of tragedy and pain his entire life, and it plays over and over in his mind. He said, "It was a hell of a day." This day will never be forgotten.

While there, he was given a 90 mm recoil, which was a rocket launcher, M16, and was pulling a lot of guard duty, protecting the perimeter from the enemy.

Being a demolition specialist, their job was to blow up trees and clear landing zones. The helicopter would hover over areas, and the soldiers would repel down between the trees with their heavy backpacks, saws, and any equipment they would need to accomplish the mission.

There were times when they were ready to blow up an LZ zone. (In the military terminology, a landing zone [LZ] is an area where aircraft can land). Often, when they tried to do their job, they were fired upon with rockets from the enemy. They would run to the right then try again to set the explosives, then run to the left. This particular time, after about five tries, some of the men went on foot to destroy the enemy that was firing upon them. The men brought back spoils of wars from the enemy, guns, and ammo, and some brought back belt buckles as souvenirs.

Going into Saigon often the Vietnamese people would get off to the side of the road and would not look the soldiers in the eye. They would turn their heads. They feared the 101st Division.

Propaganda posters were saying, "Beware of the man that carried the little black stick with the white chicken on his arm." The chicken they referred to as the American Eagle.

Larry has many sad memories, like all persons who serve in wartime; however, he also has many enjoyable moments with his fellow brothers while they too were defending the country: the USA. He knew they were doing something special for the country. He indicated, "I was proud to fight. I never feared death. If death is what it took to win for the USA, so be it."

There were some good R & R times (rest and relaxation). The 101st could not go to places a lot of the other military branches could go. The 101st would go to Eagle Beach. Eagle Beach, is in the South China Sea. The military would fly them to the beach or place them on a barge to transport them to the beach. The men would lock all of the combat gear and rifles in lockers. They were there to rest and relax, not to be on guard, fearing the enemy. The war would stop for a little while. While at Eagle Beach, it was a time of fun for three days. The navy or other military branch was there to protect the beach and their fellow soldiers.

Throughout the years, he wondered if his friend and sergeant had survived the war. After forty-nine years, he found his sergeant on social media and flew out West to visit with him.

Larry said, "It was like no time had passed. We picked up conversation and friendship where we left off forty-nine years earlier." In this case, social media played a tremendous role in reuniting a friend and fellow army brother.

During this visit, his sergeant shared that he was always afraid he would lose someone in battle.

However, during all the time in combat, he never lost anyone and had no severe injuries to his men. The sergeant was extremely thankful for their success. During combat, the company was mostly divided into groups of two to four men. Seldom was the entire company together. This is believed to have added to why there was no loss of life in our company over the four years.

The Garnet Memorial Wall in Washington, DC, erected in 1982 has 58,200 names on it, and some are his friends. He was able to come home and has lived an extraordinary life. However, he will never forget, and his heart is broken and changed by this experiences.

Researching on social media, it is said that the government ramped up the number of soldiers in Vietnam in 1965 and beyond. By 1969, it was estimated there were more than 500,000 personnel there. According to an online search, it was estimated that 1,622,973 lives were lost in the Vietnam conflict.

The conflict was between the communist government and allies known as the Vietcong against South Vietnam and the United States. The conflict was in South Vietnam, North Vietnam, Cambodia, Laos, and Southeast Asia. South Vietnam wanted to be more like the United States. It was referred to as the American War. North Vietnam wanted to unify the country under communist rule, like Russia and China (Wikipedia).

As the years and war continued, I recall that the American people were in the street, protesting the war. The costs and casualties of the war were too much for the United States to bear. The citizens of the United States were destroying property and families, fighting against one another. One believed the war was justified, another totally against it. As the soldiers were returning home, protestors would meet them at the seaports, airport, in the streets, and in restaurants and taunt and even spat upon the soldiers. There were unbelievable scenes on television as men and women arrived home from Vietnam. Imagine how you would feel if you had been in Vietnam, fighting in the 110-degree heat waves, monsoon season, mudslides enemies hiding in the brush, and you had experienced your best buddy getting killed, then returning home to the land you were fighting for and be spat upon, tormented by your American fellow man. How tragic for the men and women of the war who never received a proper "thank you."

It was a disgrace how fellow Americans treated the soldiers as they returned home from the war. Thousands gave their lives in foreign lands, and thousands are living with physical and mental challenges. My brother and other soldiers will never be the same as they were when they first left the USA to go to a foreign land to fight for the country they loved.

The US combat units were withdrawn by 1973.

Let us give our military our greatest respect. They have scares that I will never have. They know the pain and disappointment that I will never experience. They have painful stories that I will never have. I get to enjoy my freedom and blessings of this country because of my brothers and others. *Thank you*!

After returning from the military, he married and had two children. During the years of rearing his children, he often worked two and three jobs to ensure his family had every opportunity to experience the good things life had to offer.

Money and things for the family had no limits. The family lived in an upscale neighborhood, attended private schools, wore designer clothing, attended the best colleges, drove expensive vehicles, and was taught to respect others, take care of their families, work hard, contribute to society, enjoy life, and succeed in whatever profession they chose.

Later in life, after his divorce, he met the person who is his soul mate, the one he wishes he had met when he was young. They are extremely successful, and above that, they have a wonderful relationship and have fun being together after twenty-five years. They traveled the world until COVID hit the United States. Rest assured, their travels have not stopped. You will find them on a cruise, on flights, in the car, enjoying the good life and enjoying what God has given to all of us, this beautiful world.

Larry could retire and enjoy his successes; however, his hands won't let him. They were made to create masterpieces, and creating masterpieces with wood, he still does today. If you can think of it, he can make it.

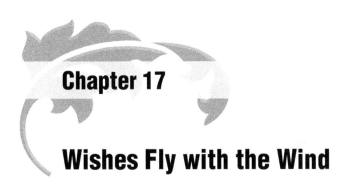

Chapter 17

Wishes Fly with the Wind

I realize more today than I did yesterday that I need to catch the wishes that fly with the wind. Only five of ten children are alive and doing well. We five will soon be gone too. The children and grandchildren will then pass on their memories to other generations.

Yesterday is gone, and tomorrow will never come. Today is all that we have. Today, as never before, let us embrace our God, our family, our friends, our homes, our nation, and our freedom.

How blessed can one family be? You see, we have a warm home to enjoy, while many are living on the streets or in broken-down homes. On this cool spring day, the usual beautiful blue sky is now covered with a cloud of gray. I see the flowering cherry trees beginning to bud, lining our three-hundred-foot driveway. I see smoke hovering low in the yard, coming from the stove, burning the pleasant-smelling wood, smoke going up the chimney and escaping into our yard. For two elderly persons, this is a real treat.

You may ask, why would that be a special treat? Well, you see, life is taking a toll on us. We knew this would occur someday, but it was always going to happen to someone other than us. We have taken good care of ourselves, ate our fruits and vegetables daily, walked miles every day, worked physical labor from early morning until late in the evening, and above all, we have completely trusted in God to keep us in good health.

> Beloved, I wish above all things that thou mayest prosper and be in health, even as your soul prospers. (3 John 2:5 KJV)

Sometimes I feel overwhelmed by our physical challenges, and then I realize many of our lifelong friends are gone on to receive their rewards. Many of them seemed to be healthier and younger than us. I then stop and remember that every day, we are shown favor by our Lord and realize our lives are in his hands.

As my husband and I have aged, and challenges have begun to happen to us, we find ourselves saying, "Why me?" Then it hits us, simply because we are human. This is just another stepping stone in life, and sometimes it comes with a heavy cross we must bear. Now that we are getting older and our bodies bend with a load of care, gathering wood for the woodstove has become a challenge for us, even though our children would gladly bring wood into the house for us if we asked.

We just find it easier to walk into the house, and up goes the thermometer to a comfortable temperature, which we do 99 percent of the time. Today I wanted to smell the wood and feel the fire heat. There is no heat like it. If you have a wood burner, I think you will agree.

Today I am looking at a large plot of ground that Tom turns over each spring and fall in preparation for planting our garden. As the temperature begins to rise this spring season, he will begin to look for the days when the sun will shine. And with his tractor and tiller attached, he will begin his yearly ritual. Up and down in that plot of ground, over and over until it is just right to his liking, and then shares, "The garden is ready for planting." Planting in the mountains is usually in late May, and often it occurs on Memorial weekend. At that time, our son would come in from Pittsburgh, Pennsylvania, and the work would begin. He works as the scripture states, "By the sweat of your brow you will eat your food until you return to the ground since from it you were taken, for dust you are and to dust you will return" (Genesis 3:19 KJV).

He does all the hard work of placing the fencing up and down the rows, where the plants can climb, which makes it easier for us to harvest as it produces those wonderful veggies and fruit. Hmm, I can almost taste those wonderful tomatoes, pepper, and, oh, that zucchini bread baking in my oven. The house is filled with the wonderful aroma that a cook enjoys so much. I see the azalea bushes in the rock garden outside this window, soon to be in full bloom. Oh, how wonderful it is to be alive and see God's handiwork one more year.

You see, "may the Lord bless you and protect you. May the Lord smile on you and be gracious to you. May the Lord show you his favor and give you his peace" (Numbers 6:24–26 KJV).

Often, when I read a book or hear a song, I wonder why the author penned this book or wrote the song. Are the words true to their experience? My words are from our life experiences as I remember or have heard from others. I began to think of the pleasures that our friends, acquaintances, children, grandchildren, and great-grandchildren have brought to my husband and me. I felt impressed to share my story with others with the hope that you can relate and be inspired to write your story. Life is a beautiful thing; however, it will end, and the legacy of each generation will linger on, only if we do not forget the past. We must learn from the past so we don't repeat it. We must share the past with the new generation. Our grandparents and family shared with us; now we are to share what we have learned and what we know.

As I remember the years, I realize our children had wonderful grandparents on both sides of the family, and now our grandchildren have wonderful grandparents too.

Today, most grandparents, such as I, work outside the home, and grandchildren spend their days in the day care centers. Finding a good day care center can be challenging; however, they are out there. You as a parent must know the curriculum they are teaching your children, even infants.

Our grandchildren called on us if they had issues to discuss or challenges with their parents, our children. They were encouraged by our children to feel free to "just ask Grandma" for advice or help. On many occasions, the grandchildren would call and be upset with their parents (our children). We would talk through the issue and come up with a plan. Needless to say, it always worked. The grandchildren would call back and say, "Mom-Mom, it worked." Amazing!

As I recall my childhood, since I was child number eight of a family of ten, I did not have a grandparent to call. As a young child, we moved to Baltimore, Maryland, and our grandparents, who were alive, were living in Virginia and New Jersey.

I could not communicate with my grandparents on the issues of the day. We had no telephone in our home. There was a telephone booth on the corner of Light Street and Montgomery Street where we lived; however, the phone was a pay phone. This meant you must have the exact change when the operator told you the cost for a three-minute call. Depending on the rate for the calling area, the call may cost you three dollars or more for a three-minute call. What guidance could you get in three minutes? How often do you think I could get Grandma's advice?

At the age of twelve, I found a real friend and someone to talk to and share my problems with. I knelt at the altar in a very large church with hundreds of people present. This kind gray-headed lady came over and knelt beside me. She said, "We are all born in sin, and I needed to ask for forgiveness." She helped me say a prayer, and it was so simple. She said, "When you go home, your family may question you being saved from your sins. You read the Bible, attend church, and find out for yourself." I did exactly as she said. It has been over sixty years, and that experience has kept me from habits, sin, destruction, depression, unfaithfulness to my husband and family, and many things I am sure I did not see or expect. This experience helped me to lead my boyfriend to Christ before we were married. And now, for fifty-eight years, both of us have faithfully served the Lord and have lived a life that is pleasing to Christ, our community, our family, and our church.

Pop-Pop, as he is called, would watch the first grandchild at his shop as our second daughter attended college and worked. He had a small baby bed in the back of his store where he worked, and there he took care of Chelsea. He would sing to her, talk to her as an adult, talk to her about the animals God put on the earth, and tell her stories about a fictitious character he called Gookinhymer. Gookinhymer could do everything but would goof up. They both had enjoyable days at what we called the shop. Daily, Pop-Pop was putting grandchildren on the school bus in the morning, bus dropping them off at his shop after school, and children were ready for pickup by their parents. He would take them out on Tuesday to McDonald's for hamburgers, fries, and drinks. All of the grandchildren were well-behaved; only one, Elizabeth, had a kicking problem. She would always swing her legs and kick Pop-Pop in the shin.

By 1993, I was working for the government outside of the District of Columbia (DC) and driving home each night to help care for the foster children that we were raising.

Remember, no one can make an impact on others like you can. Sometimes we don't realize how important we are to others until it is too late. Just think what an impact you have on this earth. No one is like you, no one looks exactly like you, no one has the same DNA as you, and no one has the same fingerprints as you. You are a special individual created by your parents and God above.

> I will praise thee, for I am fearfully and wonderfully made: marvelous are thy works; and that my soul knoweth right well. (Psalm 139:14 KJV)

If you do not have someone you can talk to, find a person. Someone you trust is often one of your family members. Sometimes it is Grandma and Grandpa that we trust and can lean upon for support, guidance, and inspiration. Sometimes it is your pastor. Sometimes it is your college, roommate. Sometimes it is a total stranger, and sometimes it is only God. Everyone needs someone to lean on in life. Find that person, and always include God!

If you are that person someone is leaning on, remember that you will not be remembered for your works but for your kind deeds (author unknown). Use every opportunity that you have as a teachable moment in every life, especially in the young impressionable life of every child.

Many rewards will come back to you and them as they mature and have families of their own. As you can see throughout this writing, and through these children, grandchildren, and extended family members, this family will be remembered for a very long time. How did we get this part of life right? With God's help and the children, Paula, Penny, Scott, and Melissa, allowing us to be a big part of their children's lives. Don't allow your life to be pressed out of measure, where you are too snappy and maybe downright nasty with your children, husband, wife, family, and friends. When you lose someone you love, you can no longer ask them the questions that you long to find the answer to. Time waits for no one, and wishes have flown away with the wind, never to return.

I now realize I am that grandma I dreamed about fifteen years ago.

Acknowledgments

I am incredibly thankful to all the family members who gave input to this book. A special thanks to the persons from Florida, Connecticut, and West Virginia, who have reviewed this writing over and over again and offered suggestions. Special thanks to my husband and children who have tolerated my absence and disconnect on occasions. I could not have done it without everyone's support in accomplishing this endeavor.

This book is dedicated to my husband; my children; my grandchildren; my great-grandchildren; my siblings Ruth, Robert, Roger, Larry; my many friends; coworkers, husbands, and wives of the children and grandchildren; and to all of the blended family members. I say to each of you, "Go forth, and do great things!"

Grandchildren, foster grandchildren, and blended family members: Chelsea, Elizabeth, Faith, Ty, Kendall, Hailee, Samantha, Reba, Gage, Amanda, Vayda, Illah, Matthew, Isaac, Kaitlynn, Aston, Morgan, Jessica, Knox, Amanda, Maverick

Sons-in-law, daughter-in-law, and grandchildren's husbands: Frank, Lee, Lori, Nate, Ben, Dora, Dan, Kenny, Chris, and Steve

Great Grandchildren: Karmendi and Kennedy (mother: Faith), Oaklyn (mother: Elizabeth), and Olivia (mother: Chelsea)

Passed with the wind: Mother, Gladys; Father, Garland; child number 1, Elvin; child number 3, Shirley; child number 4, Hubert; child number 5, Lee; child number 6, Nell

Pictures:

Garland and Gladys Payne pregnant with first child

1949 Oldsmobile; Robert Payne (age 19), Roger Payne, Thelma Payne, Ruth Payne, Nell Payne

Robert Payne, and the Mule

Sally Payne (placed in an asylum), Garland Payne, Corbin Payne, Minnie Payne

Garland Payne, Grandfather Tipton Payne

LINES OF LIFE RUN THROUGH THE MOUNTAINS

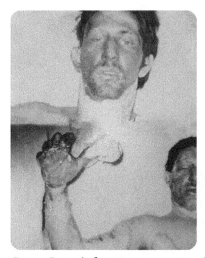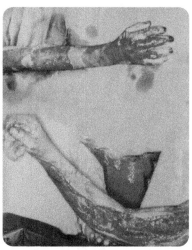

Roger Payne's four pictures were taken weeks after the burn accident.

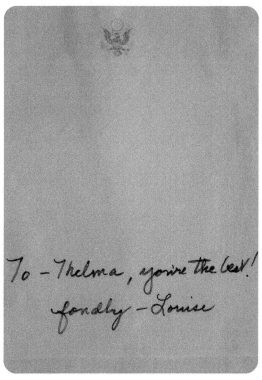

Note from a senator's wife

2016 forty-inch East Coast's snowstorm

Family of ten: 1966 *front*: Roger, Elvin; *left to right*: Nell, Ruth, Hubert, Shirley, Larry, Eddie, Thelma, Robert; three pregnant girls

Vietnam: Larry, Bronze Star Recipient

Larry Payne, 101st. Airborne Jump Training

Vietnamese Worker - 1967

About the Author

Thelma Flynn is an author and professional, who has had the pleasure of meeting leaders and dignitaries from around the world. She recalls thousands of professionals, directors of agencies, leaders of countries, presidents and leaders of the United States, senators, judges, admirals, generals, governors, writers, authors, and chief executive officers from a wide variety of cor-  porations and from luncheons at the state department to the home she shares with her husband, who is her childhood sweetheart. She is a devoted family woman and has been a proud servant of Christ since the age of twelve. She has served in every aspect of the church—from being a teacher, leader, singer, and a good listener—so she could help others by seeking answers in prayer for them. She prayed for wisdom and guidance in writing this book with the end goal of helping others overcome the challenges they may face. She is a fervent grandmother/great-grandmother/foster mother to two sisters and an earnest lover of sweet tea and hot peppers.

She embarked on her working career at age fifteen and retired from the US government in 2017. She holds many credentials in leadership, hospitality sales, management, event planning, and customer service, to name a few.

Now retired from her day job, she enjoys serving others and reading. She encourages everyone to find some therapeutic time for themselves through these avenues.

Printed in the USA
CPSIA information can be obtained
at www.ICGtesting.com
LVHW011119170824
788407LV00003B/20

9 798892 436748